Rhymes for Our Times

(Skews on the News)

Rhymes for Our Times

(Skews on the News)

Norm Levy

Salt Marsh Cottage Books, LLC
Bluffton, South Carolina

Copyright © 2009 by Norm Levy
All rights reserved

All rights reserved. No part of this book may be used or reproduced in any manner without written permission, except in the case of brief quotations embodied in critical articles or reviews. For permission, contact the author at norm@smc-books.com.

Published by
Salt Marsh Cottage Books, LLC
P. O. Box 2511
Bluffton, SC 29910
www.smc-books.com

ISBN 978-0-9770573-3-7

Printed in the United States of America

First Printing: November, 2009

Acknowledgments

Yes, I did write these verses, but it was Jane Hill—publisher, editor, designer, and friend—who made this book happen. I thank her for her work, multi-talents, patience, and encouragement. To my friends at The Literary Club in Cincinnati and the Island Writer's Network of Hilton Head Island, I extend my gratitude for their personal reactions to iterations of these verses expressed though laughter (at the right places) or groans awarded to particularly egregious or "overly-juicy" puns. And to my wife Joan—a special award as "first hearer" of these verses. Her comments and reactions provided valuable and necessary triage.

Author Comments

    Rhymes for Our Times is an anthology of light verse extensions of actual headlines that have appeared in newspapers, magazines, or on the Internet.

    Headlines, as a compressed form of communication, seem to be especially compatible with our cranked-up, quick-cut, low-attention span society. Headlines might be seen as a kind of muscular, western haiku.

    I began composing headline-inspired verse more that fifty years ago. Headlines today are a basic and continuing source of material for comedians of all stripes, as well as for news commentators. Even the venerable *New Yorker* has for years tucked at the very bottom of prose columns a provocative headline and a line or two of wry commentary. Every day, Reuters news service hosts an on-line feature called "Oddly Enough" which consists entirely of provocative headlines. The Internet edition of any newspaper or magazine is replete with long listings of headlines.

    The headlines used as easy fodder for comedians are usually those with obvious double entendres, such as "Dentist Fills Wrong Cavity" or "Woman Grows Gigantic Melons." Others involve unintended word juxtaposition, for example: "Enraged Cow Injures Farmer with Ax." Still others are references to bizarre happenings, as in: "World's Fastest Blind Driver." These are the equivalents of already composed, freestanding one-liners.

    The headlines that attract me are those that can be extended, elaborated upon, and otherwise deformed to further my personal brand of social commentary. Light verse attracts me because it is fun and challenging to write. The light verse form is also very welcoming to rhyme and word play, values brevity, and by tradition is encouraging to balloon-puncturing and ironic observation.

    Let the rhymes begin . . . .

Rhymes for Our Times

Money and Business	1
Religion	33
Government, Politics, and Law	45
Crime	63
Arts and Media	79
Sex	95
Mathematics, Science, and Environment	103
Health and Medicine	121
Food and Drink	131
Travel	147
Sports	155
Fashion	161
Animals	177
Education	189
Everything Else	195
Death	205

Money and Business

Funny money? Only if it's not yours.

Serious money? Now that's the kind that is yours. And today your money is harder than ever to acquire and keep. It's a challenge to feel secure when banks fail, hedge funds don't hedge, interest rates aren't interesting, loans are lame, and suspicious financial instruments abound with unintelligible acronyms like SIVS, REPOS, and SWAPS. The "watchdogs" don't seem to be watching either.

What could possibly be amusing about all of this? Actually, if your money is <u>not</u> in the game, it could be laughable. After all, people go to "horror movies" all the time to be amused—which is possible if you're not the victim.

The Economist June 11, 2005

The Hard Task of Reforming Nigeria's Banking System

"An increasingly popular way for banks to attract new depositors in Nigeria is to hire fleets of young women and send them around Lagos's Victoria Island business center in skimpy outfits. Many of these [so-called] 'relationship managers' complain of having to provide 'other' services to win customers . . . ."

> Most Lagos banks, to swell their coffers
> Resort to new exotic offers.
> Adjusted rates or terms extended
> Are old ideas now all upended.
> The banks must now be more inventive
> About depositor incentive.
> Smart financiers place new reliance
> On private ways to service clients.
> Recruit young staff from the nubile ranks
> Your depositors will offer thanks
> To "Managers" so hot and flirty
> While interest rates go down and dirty.

Norm Levy

USA Today: July 26, 2005

More Hotels Try Fewer Sheet Changes

"Fresh bed sheets every day aren't automatic in hotel rooms anymore.... Nearly all Hyatt hotels went from changing each guest's sheets daily to every four days.... Marriott's more upscale full-service hotels began switching to every three days...."

    For weary travelers nothing beats
    The feel of freshly laundered sheets—
    So crisp and clean and smooth and white
    A small, yet civilized delight.
    But, profit rules in corporate suites
    Involved with changing <u>balance</u> sheets.
    This should make each traveler nervous
    Abused by many cuts in service.
    When cost accountants keep the score
    Less linen change means "less is more."
    <u>Not</u> changing sheets I do assess
    As simple proof that "LESS *IS* LESS!"

The Wall Street Journal: December 28, 1994

Advertisement for Auto Lease

> "Lamborghini is bullish on leasing. Diablo VT—The Renaissance. Lease $2,999.00 a month/ $52,000 down. 1994 manufacturer's suggested retail price of $239,000."

Our highway speeds are surely teeny

For any souped-up Lamborghini.

So how to feed that raging need

For surging, heart imploding speed?

An offer still more risky yet

Just hurdle headlong into debt.

Reuters

Embarrassed GM to Rename Car With Risqué Overtones
October 13, 2003

✉ Email 🖨 Print

"General Motors will rename its Buick LaCrosse in Canada because the name for the car is slang for 'masturbation' in Quebec . . . GM officials, who declined to be named, said it had been unaware that LaCrosse was a term for self-gratification among teen-agers in French speaking Quebec . . . ."

A painful gaff for General Motors
Trying to spin its cultural rotors.
On second thought, it just might be smarter
To stay with the original charter.
Find a catchy French-sounding creation
Encouraging "auto-stimulation!"

Money Magazine. August, 2005

It's Been a Bad Year for Seers

"Bond yields were supposed to rise. THEY FELL. The dollar was supposed to fall. IT ROSE. The sectors that had led the market TOOK A BATH . . ."

Financial seers have varied disguises
Now they're short—but, tomorrow they're long
Some live on hedges, dangerous edges
But, each one is quite frequently wrong.

The market goes up, the market goes down
You are told there are no guarantees
Except for just one—YOU'll never be done
With paying commissions and fees.

Norm Levy

The New York Times: January 14, 1999

Markets Have a Funny Way Of Reacting to Reality Once They Think It Through

(A quote in an article on economic turmoil)

A market that can "think it through"!
I've never met one; think, have you?
A market can at times be funny.
I've seen one laugh—then eat my money!
If markets really think at all,
They know two things: to rise . . . then
                             F
                              A
                                L
                                  L

The Economist: April 1, 2006—"Tender Offers"

The Government of the Republic of Bulgaria Announce The Forthcoming Privatization of The National Airline Company

Bulgaria Air

"Bulgaria Air successfully operates 30 regular air-routes and charter programs due to the highly experienced and qualified pilots, skillful maintenance stuff and modem aircraft pool."

This airline's "for sale"—and do we have a deal—
It's Bulgarian Air—the price is a steal.
You get pilots and planes—if that's not enough
We'll even throw in that "maintenance stuff."

Norm Levy

The Cincinnati Enquirer: June 19, 1999

Glory of Rome Casino in Indiana To Reopen

"Caesar's Indiana expects to reopen its riverboat casino . . . two weeks after the Glory of Rome was closed due to a buildup of silt . . . beneath it . . . By law the 452 foot long, 4000 passenger boat must maneuver the river during at least part of its two-hour gambling excursion . . . The company won't say how much it lost because of the shut down."

"Dat ole man river" hates the ruse
That holds a gambling boat must "cruise"
(If only ten yards from the shore)
A scheme right out of *Pinafore.*

The river's weapons are but few—
In fact, they're limited to two—
Rising waters or heavy muck
Anathemas to Lady Luck.

Glory of Rome has bid adieu
To weeks of gambling revenue
Unaware of the river's stealth
And plots to undermine its wealth.

Investors Business Daily: December 13, 1999

Make $4000 Per Day Playing Baccarat

" . . . You can make a luxurious living playing our new advantage Baccarat system even with no prior knowledge of the game . . ."

(Advertisement in the
"Investment Opportunities" section)

An audacious twist of philosophy

Shapes the premise of this pitch

A little knowledge may be dangerous

But NO knowledge makes you rich!

Norm Levy

The Wall Street Journal: June, 1996

These Old Stogies Just Might Be Worth Some $2,000 Apiece

BALLYMOTE, IRELAND—" . . . Mr. Perceval, Lord over 1,400 sheep in a country manor called 'Tempest House,' is the surprise owner of what may be the oldest, most expensive smokable cigars in the world. The cigars, more than 600 of them, have been stashed in Mr. Perceval's cellar since the 1860s. Thanks to the mist from a nearby lake and the Irish damp, the cigars, recently unearthed, having been perfectly preserved in their own natural humidor . . . Mr. Perceval says one American investor, who wasn't identified, has offered him $1,000,000, or $2,000 per cigar, for a box of 500."

It's pure Irish wit!

I'm sure someone's joking.

At $2,000 per

Just what are they smoking?

The Economist: September 11, 1999

SENIOR CLAIRVOYANTS

(Headline in "Appointments" section)

"New, web-based financial journal seeks writers who, if not actually clairvoyant, are accustomed to thinking and writing about the next thing to happen in the markets."

Predicting markets is quite chancy—
It mixes fact and necromancy.
Now comes an ad of startling candor
Providing us a public gander
Into this truth, so pure and buoyant
The market's need for a clairvoyant!
Each complex chart replete with numbers—
Is a diversion that encumbers
This simple thought that's fun (and tragic)
The market really runs on magic!
A revelation most surprising
In financial advertising.

Norm Levy

Yahoo! News: December 15, 2001

Pisa's Leaning Tower Reopens

✉ Email 🖶 Print

". . . *Pisa's Leaning Tower reopened . . . after a decade-long renovation . . . The soil underneath its foundations began sinking before workers completed the third [of eight] levels. The builders forged ahead, however, completing it in 1360 . . . 'The tower has recovered, but like elderly people it needs treatment,' said Michele Jamiolkowski, the head of the $27 million project . . .* "

    In this world of grief and woe

    It's encouraging to know

    That even when foundations sink

    And things are at disaster's brink

    It's possible to stop a crash

    With time, resolve, and tons of cash!

The New York Times: January 28, 1999

Correction

(Noted in Business Section)

"An article in Business Day [section] on January 18 about Sam L. Ginn, chairman of Airtouch Communications, misstated his holdings of . . . options and their value . . . Mr. Ginn . . . has 2.61 million options worth $178.3 million, not 1.75 million options worth $170 million."

Apologies to Mr. Ginn

For dire journalistic sin.

The call for truth and justice mounts

When every extra million counts.

The New York Times. April 29, 1997

Mexican Executive Acquitted of Fraud

"A Federal District court judge [in Mexico City] said [the man] committed a 'mere omission' when he failed to pay five million dollars in taxes . . ."

It's fun to do business in this Mexican wonderland

And refreshing to note there's no malice in blunderland.

March 13, 1999　　　　　　　　　　*Economist*

How Dentists Sank The Shippers

"What is the connection between German dentists and the collapse of Asia's shipping industry? . . . the German government, in the early 1990s, created a tax shelter . . . that would commission new freighters . . . it was a good deal, and plenty of [so-called] 'dentist boats' were built . . . and arrived just as the Asian [economic] crisis hit . . . a record number of vessels are now headed for the scrap yards."

> This metaphor may seem banal—
> But here's a "fiscal root canal."
> This dental greed may well deserve
> A shock to dentists' "wallet nerve."
> Past bills and drills could just explain
> Why this time I don't feel their pain.

March 12, 1999   *The New York Times*

World Bank Beats Breast for Failures in Indonesia

A breast-beating bank—now that's a surprise
A bizarre anthropomorphic surmise.
Do banks have other erogenous zones?
Prurient interest? Libidinous loans?
Principle mounting or corporate assault?
It's best we leave and not open this vault.

The Wall Street Journal. March 4, 2002

Disney Publishing Unit Settles Suit Over Claim of Beardstown Ladies

"... The Beardstown Ladies, the investment club comprised of folksy, elderly investors, claimed to have beaten the market by 23.4%. ... Their book, *The Beardstown Ladies' Common Sense Investment Guide* sold about a million copies. But after *The Wall Street Journal* [and others] raised questions about the accuracy of the group's claims . . . an audit [revealed] that their average return was only 9.1% at a time when the Dow . . . went up an average of 12.1%. The Club apologized publicly and attributed the error to a miscalculation by the club treasurer . . . A class-action settlement . . . would be about $16 million . . ."

    The Beardstown Ladies sing this song

    Doo Dah, Doo Dah

    We claimed huge gains, but we were wrong

    All the Doo Dah day

    We <u>over</u> claimed somehow

    Of course we're sorry now

    Go bet your money on a bobtailed nag

    Then maybe you'll beat the Dow.

March 13, 1995 *Business Week*

Fat Price for Pudgy Gene

"... On February 28, Amgen, the biotech powerhouse, won an intensely contested auction for the right to work with an obesity gene that had been identified by scientists at Rockefeller University. Amgen will pay the University 20 million upfront for the right to the gene."

Now—lucky Amgen struts and preens
So proud of its designer genes
Yes, life is good and life is grand—
Just live off the fat of the land.

CNN.com

Negative Economic Growth
October 18, 2001

"Lawrence Lindsey, President Bush's top economic adviser, said in a speech to a Schwab Capital Markets symposium in Washington that . . . he expected 'small negative growth' for the third and . . . fourth quarters of this year . . . The technical definition of a recession is two consecutive quarters of negative growth . . . ."

What a generous term is "negative growth"
Mouthed by economists generally loath
To articulate words perceived as confession
That the economy slinks toward recession.
Lulled, I'll admit by this comforting call
I thought "negative growth" beats no growth at all.
Then reality struck—I adjusted my thinking
"Negative growth" means MY assets are <u>shrinking!</u>

The Wall Street Journal: October 25, 2001

In Picking Stocks, Monkey Outshines Big-Name Pros

"In this dark season, the carefree monkey scampered to the top perch in the investment jungle . . . . Amateurs, professionals and the monkey have now completed five rounds of competition . . . . A blindfolded monkey throws darts at a newspaper stock listing . . . The monkey is ahead . . . the professionals are next, and the amateurs are third."

There's some thing amiss in the stock market jungle
When simian gurus cause humans to bungle
Not just one time—but five times—what does this
     portend?
It's more than coincidence—it seems like a trend.
It appears that investors are clustered in clumps
There's a group you call "chimps" and a group you
     call "chumps!"

Money and Business

The New York Times: July 18, 1996

Buyer of Aids Patients Insurance Quitting

San Francisco—"A company that buys life insurance policies from aids patients so that they can get money before they die is suspending the business, acknowledging that new medicines may take away its customers. The announcement by Dignity Partners, Inc., sent its share price plummeting 77% on the NASDAQ stock market."

Fickle death—where is thy sting?

And the cash you claimed to bring?

The New York Times: July 25, 1993
(Ad in the Business Section)

> **Two British Lordships of the Manor for Sale** "We are able to offer these two very rare and valuable British titles for the immediate sale. Included are the rights as laid down by Act of Parliament and privileges enabling the purchaser to open many social and professional doors. Over 1,000 years old they're amongst the oldest titles in the world, and offer an insured investment opportunity . . . available to persons of good standing of any nationality. The prices of the lordships are U.S. dollars 19,850 and U.S. dollars 24,600, inclusive of all legal fees and transfer costs . . ."

For nineteen grand and change in cash
You, too, may don a purple sash
And sashay to some distant shire
As Lord of your petite empire.
A thousand years of proud tradition
Can now be yours (less small commission).
A check will do—if bona fide
(No plastic please, we have our pride).
Hop a train to rural station
Seek out local transportation
Hail a cabbie—he'll sound his horn
The Lord is to the Manor borne.

The New York Times: October 8, 1993
(Advertisement)

FLY A MIG 29

"...you need not be a pilot. Accompanied by a top Russian test pilot you'll take the controls of the legendary supersonic fighter with a flight plan you help design. Flight packages from $6,000..."

Beat swords into plowshares

Pruning hooks made of spears

And MiGs are for joyrides

Big red stars—souvenirs

Red Square hosts McDonald's

Where Pepsi now trickles

You get extra french fries

For hammer and sickles

Karl Marx had the insight

So did Engels, his pal

It comes down to the way

You use *Das Kapital*

The Wall Street Journal: March 12, 1993

> **Annual Las Vegas Trade Show Was Where the Thrift Shops Get Stuff in Wholesale Lots**
>
> *"This is the place to come for large rubber snakes, purple hair trolls, novelty condoms, and excess Dutch civil defense urinals . . . in earlier years, most exhibitors were surplus dealers or liquidators. Now, many sell faux surplus designed and manufactured to be sold through army/navy stores."*

When it comes to faux, how faux might you get?

Simulated, bogus leatherette?

The Wall Street Journal: February 5, 2008

Moody's Weighs Warning Labels For Its Ratings

"Credit-rating firm Moody's Corporation . . . is considering major changes in how it rates mortgage-related bonds and other securities hit hard by the credit crunch. The possible changes include new labels that would make it easier for investors to distinguish structured finance vehicles such as collateralized debt obligations from less-volatile corporate and government bonds . . ."

Can't sell it, transfer it, or park it?
Your bond is a drug on the market.
Now Moody's says soon you'll be able
To check out their new "warning label."
Every bond should be carefully viewed
For all "side effects" that might include
Wallet-pain—something sharp and acute
When your sell order won't execute.
Stomach cramps or a clutch in your throat
When the value declines on your note.
Screams that can set you on edge
When you're pushing your broker to hedge.
If "dejection" lasts more than four hours
Call your lawyer, or head for the showers.
When it comes to your personal wealth
Your bonds are a hazard to health.

The Wall Street Journal: January 8, 2008

Risk Officers Caught in the Crosshairs
Banks Look for Scapegoats

"Should Wall Street's top internal cops be thrown in the clink? . . . In the most obvious sense, many bank risk managers have failed in their task: keeping losses within predetermined levels . . . Of course, the limits of their toolkits are partly to blame . . . it is the unknown [scenarios]—like the rapid and severe subprime meltdown—that catch them unawares."

It's a comfort to know that your upstanding bank

Has safeguards in place so your nest egg won't tank.

But unforeseen error can swoop in to wisk

The disguise from the guys who claim they tame risk!

Money and Business

CNNMoney.com

Starbucks Out of China's Forbidden City

July 14, 2007 ✉ Email 🖨 Print

"After years of controversy, and a protest by one of China's most popular TV personalities, Starbucks has finally closed its door in Beijing's imperial palace . . . [the] TV anchor complained that the American chain's presence in the symbol of the Chinese nation was trampling on Chinese culture."

Now Starbucks has big trouble brewing

With coffee the cause of its undoing.

The Chinese show no hint of remorse

With "culture" not coffee grounds for divorce.

The Wall Street Journal: August 16, 2007

"Sorry" Is the Rarest of Words
Hedge Fund's letters blame losses on others

"In the past few weeks, some of the biggest names in Hedge-fund land have lost as much as a third of investors' money. None of these highly paid managers are prostrating themselves before their clients, begging forgiveness. Instead, in letters to clients, they point fingers at other hedge-funds, once-in-a-lifetime events, and their own computer programs."

> As head of the fund, I duly pledge
>
> I'm innocent of trimming the hedge.
>
> Blame it on fate—don't blame it on me.
>
> (But don't forget to pay me my fee).
>
> I get 20 percent of any gain.
>
> You—100 percent of the pain.

The Wall Street Journal: October 30, 2007

When It Takes a Miracle to Sell Your House

**Owners, realtors bury statues of
St. Joseph to attract buyers.
Don't forget to dig him up.**

"Methods for burying the statue vary. Instructions give buyers several options, including burying it upside-down next to the 'For Sale' sign."

> Prayer is good for the soul
> And may even prevail
> When invoking Saint Joe
> In a real estate sale.
>
> In seems rather odd
> That the Saint thinks it's fine
> To be buried head down
> Near a real estate sign.
>
> May he answer my prayer
> And my realtor's petition
> And I hope he'll forgive
> All sins of commission.

The Island Packet - May 9, 2009

AMID REVOLT PRICES CUT ON BIGGER BRAS

London—"Britain's largest clothing retailer, Marks & Spenser, has backed down on its incendiary policy of charging a $3 surcharge for bras that are DD or larger in the face of spreading consumer revolt. About 14,000 women gave their name to a Facebook campaign aimed at eliminating the big boob policy.

Bra buyers loudly shouted, "NO"

To prices tagged "pay as you grow."

Consumers raged while proving that

There is power in "tit for tat."

Religion

Don't you believe it! You <u>will</u> believe it! Pray this way (or maybe that way). What's it all about? Where did we come from? Where are we going? How will it all end? With these universe-sized questions still debated, there is plenty of space for both saints and charlatans. Read all about it.

Norm Levy

Religion

The Cincinnati Enquirer: February 13, 1993

Faxes Sent to God Despite Rabbi's Warning

Jerusalem—"Hundreds of people have been faxing messages to God despite a rabbinical warning that it does not replace prayer, a phone company official said Thursday. 'We have been receiving between 100 and 200 requests [a day] to plant notes to God in the Wailing Wall since the service began last month . . .'"

I wonder—does God truly care
If hailed by electronic prayer?
Is prayer pronounced by human lips
Truer than from computer chips?
Should one exclude computer hacks
Who choose to send their prayers by fax?

I'd hope—as controversy mounts
God feels that it's the thought that counts.

The New York Times: February 14, 2002

Uproar Over a Sliced, and Revered, Meteorite

"When The American Museum of Natural History opened its gleaming new planetarium two years ago, it gave its highest place of honor to the Willamette meteorite, the pitted, 15½-ton boulder that fell to earth more than 10 millennia ago . . . The meteorite has a flat spot at the top created by museum curators in 1998 when they cut off a 28-pound chunk and traded it to a private collector for a half ounce of Mars . . . [This] dismayed the Clackamas Indians of Oregon who regard the meteorite as a spiritual union of earth, sky and water."

When water, sky, and earth do clash
With institutions flush with cash
Discussions can be eons long
Sorting meteo<u>rite</u> . . . from wrong!

Religion

Forbes: December 1, 1997

Will The Last Person To Leave Please See That the Perpetual Light Is Extinguished

(Sign in vestry of a New England Church)

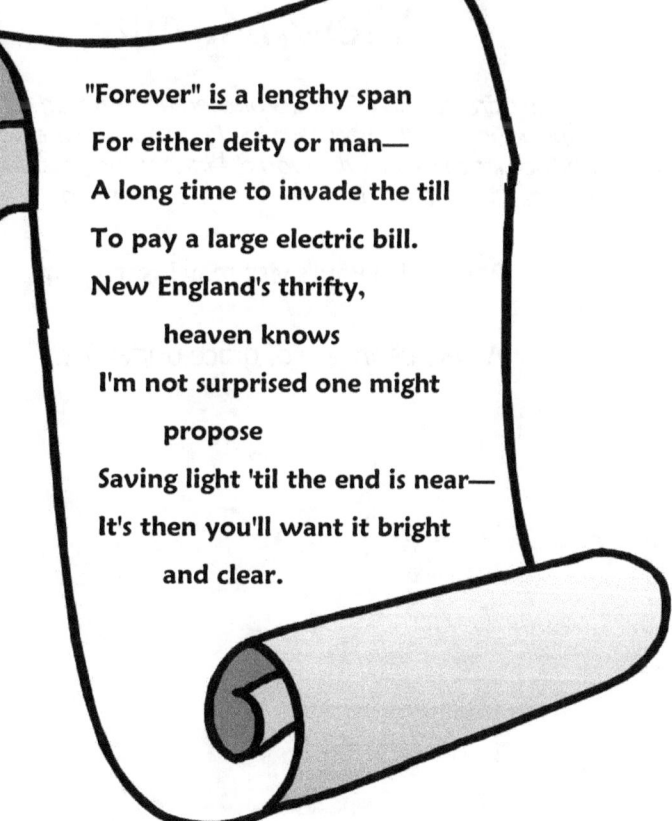

"Forever" is a lengthy span
For either deity or man—
A long time to invade the till
To pay a large electric bill.
New England's thrifty, heaven knows
I'm not surprised one might propose
Saving light 'til the end is near—
It's then you'll want it bright and clear.

Norm Levy

The New York Times

How the Pope Will View Manila

"Jaime Cardinal Sin of Manila blessed an armored car for Pope John Paul II yesterday. The Pope will see the Philippines this week through a 4-inch-thick glass bubble that can withstand grenades and machine guns."

Pope John Paul's visit may just require

A new definition of grace under fire.

Religion

The Economist: November 9. 1991

𝕾𝖕𝖎𝖗𝖎𝖙𝖚𝖆𝖑𝖎𝖘𝖒 𝕰𝖒𝖇𝖗𝖆𝖈𝖎𝖓𝖌 𝕸𝖆𝖙𝖊𝖗𝖎𝖆𝖑𝖎𝖘𝖒?

"... A church in Essex unveiled a new stained-glass window portraying a Ford Fiesta car. 'It symbolizes the church's historical links with Ford's Dagenham car plant,' explained the vicar..."

Some may find it quite distressing

(More like churchly window dressing)

A car—enshrined in tinted glass

A symbol seemingly too crass.

That Essex vicar knows his flock

For them, this icon holds no shock

They turn to scripture—where it's read

"Give us this day our daily bread."

So Essex workers praise the Lord

Saying simply, "Thank God ... for Ford!"

The Atlanta Journal Constitution: May 24, 1991

". . . Many people have said that they can see the face of Jesus, amid spaghetti and tomato sauce, on Pizza Hut billboards posted around the Atlanta area. A Pizza Hut spokesman said that unless it appeared that the billboard offended people, it would be left up until scheduled to come down . . ."

Signs and wonders may mark the way

But one wonders about a sign

Where Pizza Hut may play a part

In some ultimate grand design.

True, miracles are rare events

Perhaps in our society

The search for more eternal things

Might start with pizza piety.

Religion

> "A special religious service for broken pins and needles will be held in a Shinto shrine in Kyoto."
>
> Notice in *a Japanese newspaper:* August, 1973

The eye of a needle is closed
The head of a pin is shattered
The point of the needle is blunt
A straight pin is bent and battered.

Old pins and needles like people
Are worn down by work and repairs
At some point a pin (or person)
Requires the comfort of prayers.

Norm Levy

The New York Times: June, 1993

When Mary Is Sighted
A Blessing Has Its Burdens

"At first blush, a report of a visit from the Virgin Mary sounds like a wonderful event in the life of a local church and its community . . . [but] neighbors are worried about their lawns and property and the mayor has said police will turn people away if they perceive a threat to the public safety . . . The New Jersey incident is all following the familiar script . . . the neighbors are upset, the bishop says don't come, and they'll show up anyway."

Mary's visit or Turin's shroud

Draw the faithful, swell the crowd

But with crowds come urban pain

Perhaps it's best to pray . . . for rain!

Religion

The Wall Street Journal: September 21, 2007

Confession Makes A Comeback

Redemption Online—Confession is no longer a private matter between a sinner, a priest and God. More than 7,700 people have posted their sins on www . . .

On-line confession
Made short and sweet
Google "Sin"—Type it in—
Hit "delete."

Government, Politics, and Law

"It's good to be the king!" wrote Mel Brooks famously. And, indeed, kings were "in" for quite a few thousands years, ruling by "divine right," Louis X1V insisted. Dictators and tyrants continue to have their fair share of the market. Representative Democracy is still in the "test" phase. But no matter what the <u>form</u> of government, the bureaucrats are there. Cronies are there. Taxes are there. Wars are there. And every now and then justice is there. Governments, like personal relationships, it's hard to live with them, but it's also hard to live without them.

Norm Levy

The Washington Post: December 27, 2008

IN AFGHANISTAN, CIA GETS CREATIVE IN FIGHT FOR INFLUENCE

The Afghan chieftain looked older than his 60-odd years . . . with duties as tribal patriarch and husband of four younger wives. His visitor, a CIA officer, saw his opportunity and reached into his bag for a small gift. Four blue pills. Viagra . . . compliments of Uncle Sam . . . . The enticement worked. The officer, who described the encounter, returned four days later to an enthusiastic reception. The grinning chief offered up a bonanza of information about Taliban movement and supply routes . . . followed by a request for more pills.

How clever of the CIA

To find creative ways to pay

The leaders of each tribal clan

To fight the evil Taliban

To win those tribal minds and hearts

You first must tend their private parts

The New York Times: October 3, 1993

The Rise and Fall of Civilization According to Tax Collection

"... the dawn of a tax history is recorded on clay tablets excavated at Lagash, the city state 6,000 years ago in what is now Iraq. Little is known about Lagash, except that it instituted heavy taxes to fight a war. That war ended, but the tax burden did not lighten. On a tablet, an anonymous citizen had scratched a complaint: "You can have a lord, you can have a king, but the man to fear is the tax collector."'

The war may be civil or the
war may be Punic
But there's always a hand in
your pocket or tunic.

The New York Times: August 8, 1999

North Korea Sees Plot After Death of Gift Cows

SEOUL, South Korea— *"In an encouraging sign that relationships between the Koreas were improving . . . 500 head of cattle, a gift from Chung Ju Yung, Hyundai's billionaire founder, [were sent] to help feed the famine-stricken North . . . A year later, North Korea announced that about half the cows had died, casualties of a . . . sinister plot by South Korea's intelligence service . . . A spokesman for South Korea's National Intelligence Agency said . . . 'It is absolutely untrue that we planted any type of surveillance device on [or in] the cows.'"*

Said Chung Ju Yung, "Now, here's the plot,

We take these cows, that fart a lot,

And plant devices in their udders

To hear the North's complaints and mutters.

And as for pesky gas and mumbles

Filters will decode the jumbles.

Thus fitted up each bovine moo

Will show that this ingenious coup

Can help our South Korean sleuths

To learn more North Korean truths."

One year later, the plan's a bust—

Half the cows have bit the dust.

This spying plan has proved absurd

Surviving cows are seen—not heard.

Norm Levy

Reuters

Czechs Cut Down on Red Tape by Cutting Watchdogs
May 18, 2005

✉ Email 🖨 Print

"The Czech government has found a way to cut down on red tape: Close the bureau for streamlining bureaucracy . . . . more than forty clerks who had been assigned the job of raising efficiency and trimming fat in civil service have been let go . . ."

**The Czechs deserve a Nobel Prize
For political enterprise.
Genius forms of fine deception
Guaranteed to bend perception.
Accept the challenge to reform.
Declare a goal to scrap the norm.
Then hire staff and loudly claim
Sincere desire to change the game.
Changes make employees nervous.
Don't upset the civil service.
<u>Fire</u> those you've just now hired.
Take the credit you desired
For the jobs that you are shaving
Claimed as a gigantic saving.
Reformers meet their proper end.
The state declares a dividend.
Quirky bureaucratic gaming
Eliminates need for blaming.
All reverts to its former state
It more than just Czech . . . it's checkmate!**

Washington Globe and Mail
September 23, 1998
(Reporting a quote from *The London Observer*)

"Most global conflict can be blamed on a basic imbalance: mankind is made up of 5000 ethnic groups with only 190 countries to live in . . . "

Solutions abound—if only one dares;

Start a world contest of "musical chairs."

5000 ethnic groups marching around

Music commences—a slow, martial sound.

Then silence . . . which spurs a furious fight

To grab off the country closest in sight.

If you lose, there's no mystery—

You're lost, and as such you are history.

The more civilized way is simply to cease

Man's brutish behavior and just live in peace.

The Cincinnati Enquirer: April 25, 2002

Smokers May Be Ohio's Savior—Extra 50 Cents Per Pack Would Go To Budget Hole

"The cost of a smoke may go up in an effort to close Ohio's $1.2 billion budget deficit . . . A 50-cent increase would raise $372.9 million next year . . ."

When next you pass that lonely band

Who huddle in the cold and stand

Through rain and sleet and hail and snow

To puff their Camel or Marlboro

Remember to extend your thanks

To those within the smoker ranks

Encourage them to buy more packs

For each will help reduce your tax!

The State now shoves a begging cup

Toward smokers told to "cough it up!"

The Wall Street Journal.com: October 26, 2001

> **State May Loosen Gambling Rules To Shore Up Their Depleted Coffers**
>
> *"The post-September 11 economic softening may have an unexpected side effect: looser restrictions on gambling in a number of states . . . The New York State Legislature agreed to permit new Native American casinos . . . The deal is part of legislators' attempt to raise new revenue."*

It's a long way from Kabul to Vegas

But, there's linkage that's destined to plague us.

Moral fiber feels suddenly sodden

Much thanks to Osama bin Laden.

With more treasury balances sinking

Old objections to gambling are shrinking.

When downstate "ground zero" was burning

Upstate the "tables were turning."

CNN.com: October 18, 2001

Attention People of Afghanistan

Aid is being dropped by planes at very high altitudes. Parachutes slow their descent . . . but the bundles will still fall very fast. They may appear small, but they are in fact large and heavy. Do not stand directly below them. If you follow these instructions you will not be injured.

(Text of a leaflet air-dropped in Afghanistan preceding aid delivery)

Even "manna from heaven" in plastic containers
Require the requisite legal disclaimers!

The Cincinnati Enquirer: March 18, 1999

Helms Objects to Funding Sex-Ed in Haiti During Voodoo Ceremonies

"Sen. Jesse Helms, R-N.C., is accusing the U. S. Agency For International Development (AID) of subsidizing witchcraft in Haiti, and he wants it stopped."

The long arm of old Jesse Helms

Extends to odd, exotic realms

Where birth control and facts on sex

Draw the Senate's special hex

Voodoo priests, with vitriol

Push needles in their Jesse doll.

Norm Levy

The New York Times: June 13, 1996

Last Minor Leaves Montana Ranch Raising Hopes to a Peaceful Ending of the Stand-Off

Jordan, Montana—"Moving one more tantalizing step closer to surrender, the Freemen released the last minor in the besieged stronghold, a teenage girl... who had also told the negotiator that she was lonely and craved Taco Bell food..."

First feed the face

Then talk right or wrong

For even saintly teens

May act like wackos

Unless they've had their customary tacos.

(with apologies to Bertolt Brecht—*The Three Penny Opera*)

Free Press Journal (Mumbai, India): June 8, 1991

Mahanta Votes in Regal Style

"... The former Assam Chief Minister Prafulla Kumar Mahanta, created quite a sensation on Thursday when he came to cast his vote in a long procession accompanied by traditional musicians and singers ...."

Assam's Mahanta shows the way

To rouse the torpid masses

With songs and dance and happy play

Appeals for all the classes

So, let's rethink Election Day

(A fit task to employ us)

If we want to get the vote out

Make democracy more joyous!

Norm Levy

The New York Times: June 4, 1993

Bosnians Divide Over New Talks to Split Country

No wonder this issue cannot be decided
It's futile to split what's already divided

The Wall Street Journal: May 29, 1992

Minor Memos

Princeton economist, Alan Blinder, suggests a Constitutional amendment requiring school children to pray for a balanced budget.

Church and State have separation

In the ethos of our Nation.

For a likely debt solution

We might change our Constitution.

Declare all debt a mortal sin

Sit back and watch the bucks roll in.

Then hear the politicians bray

You have no choice—you pray—you pay!

Norm Levy

The New York Times: November 6, 2001

Budget Cuts May Foul Sidewalks of Paris

"On any given day [in Paris] you can find yourself dodging a municipal worker on a bright green motor scooter with a vacuum-cleaner hose attachment . . . homing in on exactly what you are trying to avoid—dog droppings . . . While Londoners and New Yorkers were forced to clean up after their pets or pay huge fines, Parisians have been able . . . to stare into spaces as their dogs did their business . . . A lot of rethinking has been going on . . . a new law will require the city's 200,000 doge owners to clean up after their pets . . . fines begin at $180 and go up to $420 . . ."

While walking their pets to the park

Parisian dog <u>owners</u> now bark

No longer just "staring in space"

While their pets make "deposits" in place.

Pooper scoopers and bags are a sign

Of Parisians avoiding a fine

While snarling one singular word

Which in French sounds something like "*merde!*"

Yahoo News: August, 2007

China Insists on Naming Living Buddhas

✉ Email 🖨 Print

"Ratcheting up its control over Tibetan Buddhism, China asserted the sole right to recognize living Buddhas, reincarnations of famous lamas that form the backbone of the religion's clergy . . . All future incarnations of living Buddhas must get government approval . . ."

Now, each reincarnated lama

Will be involved in heavy drama

With Chinese agents acting oddly

Who'll tell who is and who's not godly.

They'll choose the boy, the time, the venue

From some obscurant Chinese menu.

Norm Levy

The Wall Street Journal: January 30, 2008

Lawyer's In-Court Reading Gets Book Thrown at Him

"Todd Paris, a solo practitioner in Salisbury, NC, was seated on a bench in court reserved for lawyers when District Court Judge Kevin Endinger caught him reading *Maxim* magazine, according to the contempt order ... [*Maxim*] depicted prominently on the front cover ... a topless model ... Judge Endinger slapped Mr. Paris with a $300 fine and a 15-day suspended sentence ..."

Long winded speeches and boring pleadings
Led Counselor Paris to "classic" readings.
He was merely passing the time of day
While perusing some rousing T&A.
But clearly the judge deemed it mal intent—
Which affected "judicial temperament."
He saw the behavior as abhorrent.
While "Justice is blind"—the judges aren't.

Crime

Someone visiting our planet for the first time might think that humans must love crime, judging by the popularity of crime shows on TV and book sales of "murder mysteries." So what's going on? Does watching a crime show or reading about an unspeakable criminal act stroke some dark vicarious desire deep in our psyche? Or, is it somehow reassuring to see that most of the time criminals "are brought to justice" (at least in the fictional accounts). Crimes that are bungled have special appeal like some bizarre incarnation of a forensically oriented Three Stooges episode. So what about extracting "humor" from crime—it's a steal!

Norm Levy

Crime

The New York Times: August 27, 1999

BANK FIRES OFFICER FOR "GROSS MISCONDUCT"

"The Bank of New York said yesterday that it had dismissed a vice-president involved in a Federal money-laundering investigation. The bank officer . . . was fired for 'gross misconduct,' falsification of bank records, and failing to cooperate with investigators . . . She was also apparently an expert on money laundering. In June she was a featured speaker at a conference in Riga, Latvia. Her topic was 'Money Laundering: Latest Developments.'"

Students proclaim they're often weary

Of fuzzy, wishy-washy "theory."

Now, here comes one who proudly teaches.

And does <u>believe</u> in what she preaches.

It's "Money Laundering 101"

An enriching form of fiscal fun

(Until you're caught through interdiction)

Which turns belief into . . . conviction!

CNN.com

Police Find That "Holy Sand" Was Drugs
January 12, 2008

"A man dressed as a priest caught at Amsterdam's airport with three kilos of cocaine under his vestments claimed to police that his packages contained 'holy sand.'"

He crossed himself and bowed his head

Then spoke—his voice was steady.

"From 'holy sand' to pure cocaine—

  A miracle already!"

Crime

The Cincinnati Enquirer: May, 1991

> **Police Hit with Kangaroo Tails**
> Alice Springs, Australia:
>
> "'Aborigines attacked three policemen with frozen kangaroo tails and then ate the evidence,' a court was told Friday . . ."

Here's a tale for all you students
Of Australian jurisprudence
Where cops are clobbered black and blue
By frozen parts of kangaroo.
Where felons mount a strange defense
By gobbling up the evidence.
Topsy turvy?—No—its modal
In a land that's anti-podal.

Norm Levy

June 16, 1999 — The New York Times

Steal This Book: What The Bible and the Beats Have in Common

"The [popular] choice of shoplifters include The Bible as well as the works by [beat] poets like William Burroughs, Jack Kerouac, and Allen Ginsberg . . ."

There's something wonderfully perverse
When people take to filching verse
Or risking eternal libel
By nicking The Holy Bible.

For those romantically inclined
These deeds are plausibly defined;
Acts of simple desperation
By seekers of their salvation.

Those folks more legally disposed
Find simple guilt—the case is closed;
But, special merit is observed
To see <u>poetic</u> justice served.

CNN.com

Bank Branch Bandit Wears Tree Disguise
July 8, 2007

"Leave it to New Hampshire, where a bank branch was held up by a man disguised as a tree . . . . Although the branches and leaves obscured much of the man's face, someone who saw images from the bank's security camera recognized the robber and called police."

In the annals of crime who could have foreseen

A time when a robber might want to "go green."

He stated the cause of this curious whim—

"Banks have branches—I went out on a limb."

Norm Levy

Man Gets Two Years in Violin Case

(Gannett Editor's Choice Headlines)

When someone steals a violin
It's tantamount to mortal sin.
A judge feels freedom to invent
A novel form of punishment.
Put that felon on the griddle—
Face the music—pay the fiddle.
Here's a thought: why not require
The object of the thief's desire
Be ever close to his embrace
And occupy the self same space?
Incarcerate the man within
The case that holds the violin.
Does this punishment fit the crime?
Cogent question—but, here not prime.
This basic issue takes its place—
Does the prisoner fit the case?

Crime

Yahoo News

First Gunshot Victim Found in Peru

Posted on: June 20, 2007

"The first person killed by gunfire in the Americas, very likely by Spanish Conquistadores, nearly 500 years ago, was found in a burial plot near Lima, Peru."

It's now unearthed—a deadly first
That started with a musket burst
About five hundred years ago
And launched an endless bloody flow.
This hidden grave broke its silence
To tell its history of violence.

Norm Levy

The Virginian-Pilot (Norfolk, VA)

Police Kill Man to Stop His Attempt at Suicide

"A man in The Philippines was killed by police when he resisted their efforts to stop him from committing suicide...."

A suicide or homicide

Will produce the same condition

Here, the thin line of distinction

Is the matter of <u>volition</u>.

The right to be or not to be

That is the issue in dispute

It's a fine point for the lawyers

But, for the corpse, the point is moot!

The New York Times: August 29, 1993

Man Wearing Rabbit Disquise Holds Up Convenience Store

"The witness's description of a man who robbed a convenience store was a bit unusual, but then so was the robbery. The man wore a white bunny head with the face cut out and carried an ax."

There's something essentially funny

In a thief dressed up as a bunny

While the *Times* is gleefully laughing

The last laugh may be typographing

In the *Times* you don't frequently see

An odd "Q" masquerading as "G."

The New York Times: August 7, 2007

To Punish Thai Police, A Hello Kitty Armband

Bangkok—"It is the pink armband of shame for wayward police officers, as cute as can be with a 'Hello Kitty' face and a pair of linked hearts . . . 'Simple warnings no longer work,' said the acting chief of the Crime Suppression Division, who instituted a new humiliation this week for police misdemeanors . . . 'It will be very embarrassing to walk around with a "Hello Kitty" armband on your arm . . . .'"

Harsher than a reprimand
And more hated than a fine
More stinging than a truncheon blow
Or your rank in steep decline.
The sharpest pain?—An ego bruise
As Thai policemen think
There's no greater punishment
Than an armband colored pink.

Crime

The Wall Street Journal: August 23, 1993
Advertisement

If laundered dollars wash on by
Please phone your friendly FBI
If the coin you drop should be suspect
Call anyhow—just call collect.

Floss Escapee Sentenced

The New York Times: June 11, 1995

Huntington, West Virginia—"An inmate who escaped from prison using a rope fashioned out of mint-flavored dental floss drew 30 years behind bars today. He pleaded guilty ... [to] committing other crimes before and after the 1994 escape. He received five years for the last escape ...."

Here's a second-story gunsel

(Perhaps inspired by Rapunzel)

Twisting mint floss into a braid

To use as an escaping aid.

The guards are waiting there beneath

He's caught—by the skin of his teeth.

The judge says, "25 year stint,"

Plus five (we guess) for choosing mint.

Crime

The New York Times: January 3, 1994

A Vast New Scandal Is Shaking Brazilians' Faith in Democracy

Rio de Janeiro—[A Brazillian congressman] "would like you to believe that he is the world's luckiest man. To explain how he deposited 51 million dollars in his bank accounts since 1989, the congressman, whose annual salary is $84,000, told investigators recently that the answer was simple: he had won 24,000 lotteries . . . ."

The fickle wheel of fortune spins

And grinds out 20,000 wins

Twirled again by Federal spinners

4,000 times—all are winners

It's as though a sovereign nation

Repealed laws of permutation

Then again, this is in Rio

Where you live your life *con brio*

Maybe it's an aberration

Or an error in translation

Semantics can be revealing

What he calls "luck," I'd call "stealing."

Norm Levy

The Wall Street Journal: December 8, 2007

Snap-Happy Crooks Incriminate Themselves

"Camera-phones seem particularly well suited to spontaneous self-incrimination. Unlike traditional cameras, cell phones are always brought along, increasing the temptation to snap a picture and boosting the likelihood that the phone will be on or near the criminal upon arrest . . . drug dealers just naturally takes pictures of their drugs, and their money, and their significant others . . ."

Ego, plus perverse temptation

Produces self-incrimination.

Cute cell phone pictures leave a trail

Leading crooks right into jail

Proverbs 16:18 said it all:

"Pride goeth before a fall."

Arts and Media

If aliens landed in any major city on a busy street at midday, they might wonder why so many humans seem to have their hands clasped in front of them clutching some small rectangular object which commands their rapt attention. Or, why do others, walking briskly in broad daylight, hold a similarly small object tightly to their collective ears while moving their lips. The media, in all of its electronic manifestations, have our world in its grip and thrall. The graphic arts too, have left the former comfortable world of two generally static dimensions to leap into the digital universe of fragmentation and movement. Something funny here?

In truth, it's too early to tell.

Arts and Media

USA Today: July 15, 1995

Miss America Wants Swimsuits Dropped

"The reigning Miss America has an opinion on whether or not contestants should wear swimsuits in this year's pageant: She's against it no matter what the public thinks . . . NIC Entertainment chief Warren Littlefield confessed he supports keeping swimsuits in for the tradition's sake . . . It probably won't hurt ratings either."

From the mouth of babes—a wrong surmise

When swimsuits drop—the ratings rise

Norm Levy

The Wall Street Journal.com

Press Release Disclaimer

> "This press release contains certain forward-looking statements identified by use of . . . terminology such as 'may,' 'will,' 'expect,' 'intend,' 'anticipate,' 'estimate,' 'predict,' 'plan,' or 'continue.' . . . These by their nature are subject to risks and uncertainties."

Ratchet your mind up to a high alert

Call out the "grammar police"

Keep you "parsing tools" nearby

When reading a press release.

It may not say what it seems to say

Leaving but these actions for us

An eye on the dictionary

Hand on a handy thesaurus.

Arts and Media

Various Headlines in *The Cincinnati Enquirer*
December 2, 2001

Weekend Suicide Bombings Kill 25

Bombing Heavy Near City

Taliban Pinned Down

Bombers Fall In Clash of the Saints

(These latter Bombers are from St. Xavier battling St. Ignatius)

Whose bombers, what clashes, and which saints?
In this world of diminished restraints
Self-proclaimed "saints" may be "sinners"
And losers transformed into "winners."
Where "Bombers" are boys from St. Xavier
Displaying aggressive behavior.
While "Bombers" with bombs fill the pages
With news of their latest outrages.
And "Bombers" rain death with great science
To the joy of the Northern Alliance.
Our world is a place of confusion
It's hard to sort fact from illusion.

Psychic Friends Network Files For Bankruptcy
Jet: February 23, 1998

"The parent company of The Psychic Friends Network, which was once the No. 1 infomercial on TV, recently filed for Chapter 11 bankruptcy protection. The company . . . listed liabilities of $26 million and assets of $1.2 million when it filed for Chapter 11 . . ."

>I doubt that costs of competition
>Explain our Psychic Friends' condition.
>Two thousand seers with special magic
>Missed the signals—to me that's tragic.
>Their lame excuses just seem numbing—
>Real psychics would have seen it coming.

"What's New in Washington?": October, 1998
(Event Notice)

> ". . . Elvis [pictures] on velvet, paint by number canvases, and other questionable works from the Museum of Bad Art . . . through October 18 . . ."

An edifice to horrid taste
Seems criminal (though crimeless)
It's note entirely a waste
It proves: <u>bad taste</u> is timeless!

The Cincinnati Enquirer: March 26, 1999

Lewinsky Visit to Russia Canceled

I feel my head might just explode
From information overload
A steady, often mindless, stream
From TV, print and magazine
From e-mail, fax and talk-show host
Of pseudo-news and much compost.
Must every factoid be reported?
Surely more might be aborted.
Monica's Russian trip is <u>ended.</u>
Would you be at all offended
If zero space or time was spent
On this non-occurring-non-event?

The Cincinnati Enquirer: February 12, 1998

Afghan Quake Victims Vastly Outnumber Supplies

Rustaq, Afghanistan—
Thousands of people huddling against the cold, over-whelmed aid-workers reaching earthquake-wracked north-eastern Afghanistan . . . with supplies too meager to ease the enormous suffering . . . Villagers from . . . tiny hamlets gathered on a cliff to watch a Red Cross aid convoy approach. They quickly realized that their suffering was far from over. The convoy consisted of only <u>one</u> car full of supplies . . . and <u>three</u> cars bringing reporters."

Through eyes of the starving one might see

"The Press" as feeding on their misery.

Peasant throngs from desperate quarters

Cast hungry eyes on plump reporters.

The Cincinnati Enquirer: December 25, 2001

The Most Overrated Books of 2001

#3 FURY by Salman Rushdie [Random House] "This novel proves what may have been suspected all along . . . If certain Islamic radicals hadn't put out a 'fatwah' (death sentence) on Mr. Rushdie, nobody outside his family would ever read his turgid, confusing fiction."

From something "bad" came something "good"
(A fact not clearly understood)
Promised death and mystic's curses
Bestowed upon "Satanic Verses"
By Mullahs and madrasa dwellers
Turn turgid prose into best sellers!

Wall Street Journal: May 17, 1996

Jumbo Paintings Become White Elephants

"Big art is big no longer. Sure, sprawling canvasses have been the hallmark of the contemporary art scene, their grand scale matched only by the prices they once fetched . . . but fashion has changed . . . during the inflated 1980s 'size didn't matter,' because buyers simply stored paintings while they waited for prices to rocket higher. Now collectors are buying to hold again, and how readily a painting will fit into a living room is something 'we factor in' when valuing it."

Now "off the wall" art is now off the wall
The bigger they come the harder they fall!

Norm Levy

The New Yorker: September, 1993

Obsessed in Rio

From an article entitled: "Obsessed in Rio—Fact Mingles with Fantasy on TV Globo, Where One Soap Opera Begets a Real-Life Murder, and Another Helps Bring Down a President"— a description of some of the key real-life players:

"They were simultaneously obsessed with and paranoically suspicious of each other, and in an attempt to seal their love in a way that might be truly binding they had each other's names tattooed on their persons—she on her bikini line, and he on his penis."

True love is a complex, confounding emotion
Conducive to baroque displays of devotion
Why else would a man take a customized stencil
And tattoo her name on his penile utensil?
In the hope that the sight might unshackle fetters
When exposed (we assume) in upper-case letters.

Arts and Media

Time Magazine: September 9, 1929

Milestones—

Married: Ruth Elder, 24, Trans-Atlantic Air Passenger and Walter Camp, Jr., in Manhattan

---

It was a simpler Time
That spared the space to cite
As worthy of our notice
This bird's pre-nuptial flight!

Associated Press: January 10, 2007

Miss New Jersey USA Reportedly Resigns

Trenton, New Jersey—"Another Miss USA tiara is changing heads. Miss New Jersey USA has resigned because she is pregnant."

The exchange of tiaras is not

an exception

It's just another unfortunate

Miss conception!

Arts and Media

The Economist: October 30, 2004

Sex Doesn't Sell

"... though life may be increasingly exciting for the sex-obsessed, in the wider population, advertisers are finding that sex no longer sells the way it used to . . . people are looking for things that are more real, more wholesome, more pure . . ."

The shocking thing in decades hence

Will be to see our innocence!

International Herald Tribune: June 6, 1991

Excerpt from an editorial

Calcutta—". . . India has pioneered a semantic revolution which glosses over reality in this country of more than 850 million people. For instance, famine has been banished from lexicon, if not life. The rains might fail, crops dry up, and people die of hunger, but they are victims only of 'scarcity.' Newspapers in India have done away with riots. No matter how many people might be killed, headlines speak only of a 'stir.' Criminals have been sanitized as 'anti-socials' and it enables New Delhi to display 'flexible rigidity' in dealing with separatist movements . . ."

Don't you see the brilliance in stupidity . . .

    Yes, I think I do!

Don't you see the courage in timidity . . .

    Yes, I think I do!

Don't you prize the darkness in lucidity . . .

    Yes, I think I do!

Then you'll appreciate "flexible rigidity" . . .

    I will?

Sex

If Elizabeth Barrett Browning's poem "How Do I Love Thee?" were classified on a new Internet search engine, it might appear as an entry between the *Kama Sutra* and <u>YouPorn.com</u>. While the cultural context and language of sex may change, nothing much has really changed—witness the colorful frescoes on the dining room walls at Pompeii. Yes, we do know a lot more about the chemistry, physiology, and psychology of sex. Writers and artists continue to generate a tsunami of words and pictures—the profound and the profane. And what has love got to do with it? Lots, if you're fortunate. But hormones keep bubbling quite independent of our limited ability to describe their effects.

Sex

Daily News: October 12, 2008

Prostitution Has Not Suffered Drop-Off Despite Economic Slow Down

"The plunging Dow Jones and panicky investors are hardly a problem for the world's oldest profession where business is still brisk.... Business has suffered a bit in the fiscal crisis... some clients are cutting back on their spending...."

A banker seeking diversion

From Wall Street's fiscal perversion

May find himself down on his luck

And chasing more bang for his buck.

The New Yorker: April 16, 2007

The Annals of Transport
There and Back Again
The Soul of the Commuter

"Commuting makes people unhappy, or so many studies have shown. Recently, the Nobel laureate Daniel Kahneman and the economist Alan Krueger asked nine hundred working women in Texas to rate their daily activities, according to how much they enjoyed them. Commuting came in last. (Sex came in first) . . . ."

Does one require a Nobel prize

To re-discover the non-surprise

That "sex" would outrank "a long commute"—

A finding I think beyond dispute.

To me, the data is simply showing

That "coming" is better than "going."

Sex

The New York Times: October 4, 1993

Pregnant Cheerleaders Bring Turmoil

Hempstead, Texas—"A fourth of the school's 15 cheerleaders were discovered pregnant this fall . . . it also confronted girls with one of the harsher facts of life: football players do not become pregnant, but cheerleaders do. No action has been taken against the fathers because school officials say they have no way of legally proving who they are . . ."

It's sad—now that they know the score
There's nothing left worth cheering for!

New York Times: August 16, 1996

In Kiosks of London Card Game Gets Dirty

London—"Having tried for years to persuade prostitutes to stop littering telephone kiosks with small cards advertising their services, Britain's telephone company has decided to crack down on the likes of 'Domination Mistress Nancy' and 'Cuddly Elana' . . .

"A new task force of inspectors will note down the telephone numbers . . . enter them in a computer and issue the prostitutes an order to stop displaying their numbers. A week later any prostitute still posting the ads will have his or her incoming telephone calls blocked."

Creative ways designed to vex

Purveyors of illicit sex

Will only spawn new deviation

"Premature communication."

Sex

USA Today

Charles and Diana Kiss Goodbye

"... James Hewitt, the cavalry officer who wrote a book about his alleged affair [with Princess Diana] told the London Sunday Times: 'I regret anything at all was written. I think to myself, What am I going to do for the rest of my life? I'm only good at two things, horses and sex.'"

Rein in your whining Captain Hewitt

Engage your brain and then intuit

Just where your skill sets intersect

It's there you'll find a job prospect

"Horses and sex" by this accounting

Suggests a common calling—mounting!

The New York Times: August 15, 1999

Don't Forget to Floss

"What's the perfect accouterment for a date in the 1990s? How about a 'Get Lucky Pak'—a wallet-sized package offering a <u>LifeStyles</u> condom and a sample of new <u>DentalDots</u>, dime-sized pads soaked in mint toothpaste with an adhesive backing to adhere to the index finger for a quick cleaning."

Sex at the end of the twentieth century

Is blatant, brazen, and often adventury.

Is this good . . . is this bad . . . hopeful or piteous?

One positive thing . . . it seems more fastidious!

Mathematics, Science, and Environment

DNA, lasers, black holes, quantum mechanics, nanotechnology, molecular biology all seem, at first, like "heavy" subjects for light verse. But DNA helps explain your arthritic knee and your ditzy uncle. A laser can shoot down a satellite, but a laser can also remove graffiti from a schoolyard wall and vaporize unsightly blue veins on your thigh. If we look for the humanity in science, there will always be a light side and the possibility of distilling a wry smile.

Mathematics, Science, and Environment

The New York Times

JET LAG—ENGINE TROUBLES PUT GE BEHIND IN RACE TO POWER NEW 777s

"As a new Boeing 777 took off on a test flight near Seattle on May 4, one of its engines back-fired in a spectacular display of belching flame and smoke.

Then on May 30 in Villaroche, France, a dead bird was fired at the same model jet engine's blades to simulate a bird-strike, with triple the number of blades damaged.

Last Friday, engineers fired another bird at GE90 engine blades in France. This time the engines passed muster, losing only one blade. So Boeing may persuade the FAA to resume agency certification testing."

> It seems strange that to test a jet motor
> One shoots a dead bird at its rotor.
> Yet, it's worth all the roar and the whooshing
> A bird in hand <u>is</u> worth two in a bushing.

Norm Levy

Yahoo News

Experts Solve Mystery of Unpopped Popcorn

Posted on: Thursday, 21 April 2005

INDIANAPOLIS - " . . . Nuisance kernels (known as 'old maids') kept many a dentist busy, but their days may be numbered. Scientists say they now know why some popcorn kernels resist popping into puffy, white globes . . . . It turns out that there is an optimal hull structure that allows kernels to explode, and leaky hulls prevent the moisture pressure buildup needed for the kernels to pop."

Many things lack explanation.
War and death and conflagration.
The human mind keeps seeking truth
To save a soul or guard a tooth.
We savor truth where we can find it
Praising experts who define it.
While new ideas wait to be born
I'll just relax—and pop some corn.

Mathematics, Science, and Environment

The New York Times: November 29, 1994

> ## Astronomy Crisis Deepens as the Hubbell Telescope Sees No Missing Mass
>
> "'It's a fairly embarrassing situation to admit that we can't find 90 percent of the universe,' said Bruce H. Margon, an astrophysicist at the University of Washington in Seattle. 'Identifying the nature and amount of dark matter is a central problem in cosmology today. It's an obsession of everyone concerned.'"

I'd expect to feel some anxiety

If I misplaced 90 percent of <u>me</u>.

There'd be angst and statistical terror

I couldn't ascribe to rounding error.

A <u>universe</u> lost—I just don't mind it

But, for science sake, I hope they find it.

Norm Levy

Flint, Michigan Journal: December 5, 1990
Crater May Be Smoking Gun In Dinosaur's End

This irritant might even vex

A large Tyrannosaurus Rex

Echoing the painful chorus

Of the sorest Brontosaurus.

The New York Times: November 25, 1998

Postal Compost

" . . . The Dallas-Fort Worth post office is trying to compost some of its junk mail problem away . . . the post office hopes to sell about 500 tons of undeliverable junk mail—mostly mail-order catalogs—to a composter which would sell the finished product to gardeners . . ."

Mary, Mary, quite contrary
What makes your garden grow?
It's compost paste from postal waste
And catalog seeds I sow.

Mary, Mary, it's moist and airy
Your vegetables are green
So good for lunch, such snappy crunch,
May I munch on L. L. Bean?

Mary, Mary, I'm rather wary
So humbly beg your pardon
What's that growing? What's that showing?
Your Victoria's Secret garden?

Norm Levy

The New York Times: July 27, 1993

The Beleaguered Dinosaur Institute Keeps Digging

". . . New T. Rex is found as a dealer fights the Federal government . . . A welter of ambiguous and sometimes conflicting laws and rules on collecting fossils has often placed professional paleontologists and amateurs in relationships of questionable legality . . . before this is all sorted out, it's quite likely that the case will end up in the Supreme Court . . . ."

Chipped and chopped from ancient rock

Then shoveled on an auction block.

All for science?— Well, I doubt it.

All for cash?—No bones about it.

For even great Jurassic jaws

Cannot protect from arcane laws.

Litigation never ceases

So these bones won't rest in pieces.

Mathematics, Science, and Environment

The New York Times: March 25, 1999

On the Horizon: A Way to Write in Thin Air

"The [new] pen called Smart Quill, will feel in the hand like a typical ball-point, but it will contain motion sensors that will record every movement a hand makes as it writes. To translate these movements into digital text, users will dip the pen into an electronic inkwell connected to a PC . . . users can even write in the air."

And . . . Future models will send a shock to jolt you out of writer's block!

Norm Levy

July 27, 1999   *The New York Times*

Agency Will Ask Congress to Drop Gasoline Additive

"Ingredient that was meant to clear the air has been found to pollute the water..."

Such good intentions gone astray

In an environmental way.

Another sad improvidence

Of unintended consequence.

If you can't breathe it, you'll drink it—

Neat paradox don't you think it!

Mathematics, Science, and Environment

Yahoo News

3/3/09: Math Fans To Celebrate Square Root Day

Posted on: Tuesday, 3 March 2009

"Dust off the slide rules and recharge the calculators. Square Root Day is upon us. The math-buff's holiday, which occurs nine times each century, falls on Tuesday-3/3/09 (for the mathematically challenged, three is the square root of nine)."

In changing times of grief and woe

With income, jobs, and stocks so low

It's vital that we try to find

Assurance of a different kind

A sure thing for eternity—

The square root of 9 is <u>always 3.</u>

Norm Levy

Scientific American, September, 1993

"Those who adore Brazil nuts have no doubt wondered why shaking a can of assorted kernels always brings the large ones to the top . . . now a team of physicists from the University of Chicago reports that it has discovered a mechanism entirely different from previous explanations . . . interest in the results extends beyond nut-maven circles. The findings could help the pharmaceutical, construction, and agriculture industries . . . elucidate the motions of landslides, avalanches and magnetic flux lines in super conductors."

The truth may appear in nutty disguises

When searching for wisdom—

                    expect surprises.

Mathematics, Science, and Environment

The New York Times: April 25, 1996

Yeast Gene Map Promises Clues to Human Diseases

"Leaders of an international team involving more than 70 labs announced yesterday they had deciphered the complete genetic structure of Bakers Yeast . . . .

The reason yeast is important is that 'virtually all the genes in yeast are also in humans'. . . 'biologists for centuries have been sinking into a quicksand of ever greater complexity' . . . but with the complete blueprint of a yeast cell, biologists have in a sense touched bottom."

The lowly yeast cell gives way

Its recipe for DNA.

Grease the pan of speculation

Look for rising expectation.

Sift the mix for richer queries

Slice off sodden half-baked theories.

The Cincinnati Enquirer: May, 1996

Fly Has Longest Sperm

The Associated Press—New York: "What creature makes the longest sperm? Forget the elephant or the whale; it is, of all things, a fruit fly.

The tiny Drosophila Bifurca cranks out sperm that are about 2.3 inches long. That's 20 times as long as the fly itself and about 1,000 times longer than human sperm."

Do female Drosophila wince or sigh

When in the presence of an unzipped fly?

The New York Times: November 28, 1995

Odd Microbe Survives Vast Dose of Radiation

"Government scientists report an astoundingly hardy bacterium that seems able to repair damage to itself that would instantly destroy almost anything else. . . . One problem researchers have faced in studying these organisms is the rarity of radiation-resistant bacteria in nature . . . They have all been been found in out-of-the-way places: in the feces of some elephants and South American llamas, in some samples of Swedish underwear, in Antarctic rocks, and in water tanks used as shielding against lethal radiation from pieces of cobalt-60."

Science, it seems, comes up with aces,

When searching in the strangest places

Like llama dung or underwear

For bugs that seem to self-repair.

To hearty souls with gamma beepers

I say, "Well done"—and finders keepers!

Norm Levy

The New York Times: April 21, 1996

Maker of Powerful Military Lasers Builds a Weapon That Can Obliterate Graffiti

"Lawrence Livermore Laboratory, builder of lasers powerful enough to shoot down missiles or ignite miniature hydrogen bombs has created a portable laser that is said to be able to obliterate graffiti from walls and statues at lightning speed. The laboratory is trying to convert many technologies developed for military purposes to commercial uses."

It seems spectacularly absurd

To think a four-letter word

Blasted into gaseous phase

By billion dollar laser rays.

I suggest an inward turning

One apocalyptic burning.

A searing zap into the core

Of that real obscenity—war.

Mathematics, Science, and Environment

The Wall Street Journal: May 1, 1991

Excerpt from a Book Review of
Lonely Hearts of the Cosmos
by Dennis Overbye

"... In 1919, Edwin Hubble discovered that the farther a galaxy was from the earth, the faster it was moving away from us; from this it followed that space was expanding in every direction and at every point. The hypothesis that this expansion could be traced back to a primordial cataclysm was confirmed in 1965 when two scientists at Bell Labs accidentally picked up a uniform microwave hiss that seemed to proceed from every region in the universe. Although they first suspected that this was caused by pigeon droppings on the antenna, it turned out that what they were hearing was nothing less than the echo of the Big Bang . . . ."

**I'd like to think the angels sang
The very moment of Big Bang
One great hallelujah chorus
Marking this occasion for us.
To learn that this sublime event
Might be confused with excrement
Led at first to gross invective
(Later, more mature perspective)
For even though it seems extreme
There's truth in that absurdist dream.
Perhaps that strange persistent hiss
Is there so we remember this
Observed from <u>sub-atomic</u> view
Those droppings look like me . . . or you!**

Norm Levy

Excerpt from the book *Machiavelli* by Ron King

(describing Machiavelli's likely meeting with Leonardo Da Vinci to discuss the building of fortifications)

"Leonardo, later worked for the Sforza Court . . . designing [though not actually building] military hardware such as crossbows, machine guns . . . and even a four-wheeled tank armed with cannon and sheathed in metal plate. He also studied ballistics so cannonballs could be aimed more accurately at the enemy. Somehow he [Leonardo] managed to find time amid all these activities to paint *The Last Supper* and invent the first toilet seat."

Eternal fame has been justly bestowed

On Da Vinci's art, his genius, his code.

Additional praise is certainly owed

For his most "touching" design—the commode.

Health and Medicine

"Healthy, wealthy, and wise" is the great trifecta in the race of life. But any encounter with being seriously <u>un</u>well snaps you into the clearest understanding that "healthy" is prime. We are simply lucky to live in a world of expected and realized medical miracles—at least one a day if the popular press is to be credited. But, life expectancy has been truly extended; bones can be mended, organs transplanted, arteries reamed, and many (but not all) scourges and plagues controlled. Yet the health slate is far from totally clean. Germs and viruses fight back with new permutations. The flu has not flown and extended life exposes new weak spots in the human corpus. Always, like lurking jackals, the quacks, the charlatans, the false prophets probe for opportunity. Health fads arise suddenly and then disappear into a cloud of broken promises and false hopes. A hearty laugh may never be a "cure," but it might help brighten the gloomy times. To your health!

Self Magazine: September, 1995

Who Would Have Thought Bagels Could Be Dangerous?

"Emergency medicine departments on both the east and west coasts report that one of the most common lacerations treated in the emergency rooms is caused by people slicing their hands instead of their bagels."

The bagel has not sense nor wit

To cut the hand that slices it.

By projection (or finagle)

It draws blame—the passive bagel.

"It's dangerous," the press alleges

This doughy blob with no sharp edges.

I toast the bagel (not with fire)

But, with respect it should inspire.

And though the bagel stands convicted
Our wounds (in truth) are <u>self</u>-inflicted.

The New York Times: April 14, 1996

Researchers Link Income Inequality to Higher Mortality Rates

"... A new study [undertaken by three faculty members of the Harvard School of Public Health] suggests that greater inequality of income contributes to higher overall mortality rates . . . 'We found that income inequality increases death rates at all ages, from infant mortality to death in the elderly.'"

This ugly fact is so unforgiving—

You can die from <u>not</u> making a living.

Health and Medicine

The New York Times: August 27, 1992

Study Says Babies Have Math Ability

"'At first blush, it seems far-fetched that infants could recognize simple numbers in math,' said Dr. Lewis Lipsitt, a developmental psychologist, Brown University. 'But now in view of a number of corroborating findings, it makes sense.'"

If you've ever changed a diaper

Then it is hardly news to you

That the tiniest of babies

Knows Number One and Number Two.

The Wall Street Journal: June 6, 1996

Growth Industry

How a Risky Surgery Became a Profit
Center for Some L. A. Doctors

Penile Enlargements Appeal to Physicians
Limited by Managed-Care Plans

Now you've heard report of it

Here's the long and short of it.

Some men are quite demanding

On issues of their standing.

Health and Medicine

The Cincinnati Enquirer: July 18, 1993

Circumcised Foreskin Used in Wounds Test

"Researcher says tissue better than skin grafts . . . because newborn skin contains fewer cells that can cause tissue rejection than adult skin, and it might result in less scarring. 'We are taking things that are thrown away anyway and trying to salvage them . . .'"

Now here's a new recycling mode

It's from the old Mosaic code

What's old is new, what's out is in

How's that for foresight—and foreskin?

The Wall Street Journal, December 9, 1996

Worth A Trip: Cut-Rate Dentures Lead to the Ozarks

" . . .There are those who might consider it odd to travel 4,000 miles for new dentures, but Charles and Amy Russell aren't among them. The Russells live in Evansville, Wyoming. Twice in the past month, they have made the two-day drive to this little Ozark town so he could have work done at the Mid-America Dental Clinic, a big discount denture operation here. A Wyoming dentist had quoted Mr. Russell a price of more than $2,000 for new dentures, including related work. The dentures here came to $335 . . ."

To save big cash, just head on South

News travels fast, by word of mouth

Brand new teeth <u>and</u> travel venture

Can be yours without in-denture

Health and Medicine

CNN.com

Phones Dirtier Than Toilets
July 14, 2007

"Your cell phone may be doing more than just making a call. It could be making you sick . . ."

Here's morbid news designed to shock us

About that deadly staphylococcus

Now lurking on each phone display

Prepared to steal our health away.

The Feds, those stealthy cell phone stalkers

Will find we all are dirty talkers!

The Daily Mail Online: October 24, 2006

Men Who Use Mobile Phones Face Increased Risk of Infertility

"A new study shows a worrying link between poor sperm and the number of hours that a man uses his handset . . . Doctors believe that the damage could be caused by the electromagnetic radiation emitted by the handset or the heat they generate . . ."

Men must take care to protect their cojones

From evil effects of cellular phones!

Food and Drink

"First feed the face, then talk right and wrong; for even saintly men may act like sinners unless they've had their customary dinners." This is a great quote from Marc Connelly's English translation of lyrics from *The Three Penny Opera*. "Feeding the face" expresses the basic biologic need that is the starting line for an immensely long and twisty culinary roadtrip that eventually leads to the land of extravagant and delicious excess. Eventually, travelers find themselves in the country of "the foody," where the tastiest fun bits are to be found. So pop the cork on any one of your personal choice of eighty-seven vintage Chardonnays and savor any two of the 382 choices on the cheese cart. The nice thing is that entry into "The Democratic Republic of Food" may only require that you have in hand a Big Mac and a Coke. But, leave room for dessert—usually something slightly bittersweet.

The New York Times: April 15, 2001

Is Nothing Sacred?

"The Bible Bar . . . a new candy bar with ingredients inspired by Deuteronomy 8:8 . . . 'A land of wheat and barley, of vines, fig trees and pomegranates, a land of olives, oil and honey.' . . . The result is a somewhat sticky granola bar that offers immediate health benefits by inspiring you to brush your teeth . . . ."

A bite into a Bible Bar

(An action very secular)

Is more than sweet gastronomy—

It's sampling Deuteronomy.

But, if the Bible Bar should fail

I prophesy a different sale—

A franchise chain of Bible Bars

Serving wine in earthen jars,

Oasis pictures, potted palms

Fortune cookies stuffed with psalms.

Where customers may drink and dine

Sipping blessed fruit of the vine.

Non-drinkers too, may wish to go

The wine can change to H_2O.

Wall Street Journal: June 23, 1993

The Screech of Tires Means a Tasty Meal For This Rural Chef

Aberdeen, North Carolina—"'They don't get freezer burn if you leave the fur on,' Mr. Squire explains. His wife glares into the open freezer at the critter, which looks surprisingly chipper, considering that her husband had found it dead on the highway. 'Whether you get it with a gun or Goodyear, it's still the same meat,' says Mr. Squire."

"One for the road" has new meaning

In this new age form of gleaning

The road-crossing chicken that died

May find itself roasted or fried

As cuisine—it's simply woeful

More to the point—**simply offal**

Food and Drink

The New York Times: December 6, 1995

Tomato Sauce in Pizza May Be Anti-Cancer Agent

"Men who eat at least ten servings a week of tomato-based foods sharply reduce their risk of developing prostrate cancer, Harvard University researchers reported today."

A joyous cry of "mama mia"
As pizza joins pharmacopoeia
When ordering you now may answer:
"Cheese, double sauce—hold the
    cancer!"

Norm Levy

The New York Times: January 6, 1996

In France's Finest Restaurants, A Slight Taste of Wrongdoing

PARIS—"A hoax, the stink of corruption in the kitchen, even a possible death by arson; these are troubled times at some of the finest restaurants in France.

An investigating magistrate confirmed reports on Friday that he had 30 chefs under scrutiny for possibly taking kickbacks from a wholesale fish dealer. Lawyer Gilles-Jean Portejoie, said that the practice was 'traditional' and the amounts were extremely modest—'a sort of tip.'"

> If your bouillabaisse seems oddly fishy
>
> It's not an error of omission
>
> The fault is not the recipe
>
> But an error of commission.

Decanter Magazine: September, 2001

Domain Saint Jemms Michelas

(Wine tasting for Crozes-Hermitage and Hermitage wines for 1999)

"Quite rich, succulent, peppery . . . with some complexity. It is old-fashioned and chunky . . . has ample fruit . . . Odd nose of rubber tires . . ."

"Rich" is good and "chunky" too

I'm pleased the fruit is ample

"Old-fashioned" is no taboo

I'd gladly down a sample..

That "odd nose" or that "rubber nose"

Suspends my wine desires

Before I'd sip I'd propose

Replacing all the tires.

Norm Levy

The New York Times: February 14, 2002

Fish Need to Relax to Taste Better

Athens, Greece—"It's a stressful job, living in a fish tank and waiting to be grilled . . . Fish living in water tanks under artificial lighting tend to suffer stress and depression [according to the] Athens Geoponic University. This changes the way that fish taste . . . To make them taste better, customize water tank color to species, provide "play time," and improve the quality of their food."

For each fish that is broiled or fried
There are issues of "taste" and of "pride."
Before donning it's thick coat of batter
There are things that, to fish, really matter.
Do not hope for a succulent morsel
If there's tension in gill or in dorsal.
And fillets won't be tender or flaky
If fish psyche is stressed-out or shaky.
So if you yearn for sweet delicate taste.
Do not feed fish on pellets or paste.
Some piscine compassion is the goal.
Even flounder has a fillet of . . . soul!

Ingredient label for an herbal tea

> "Blackberry leaves, lemon grass, spearmint, rosehips, orange peel, saffron, ginger, citric acid, and the mumbled chantings of a certified tea shaman."

While labels may confuse a layman
It's good to know a <u>licensed</u> shaman
Chants syllables into my tea
Presumed of benefit to me.
Before my stomach starts its rumbling,
I'd like to know just what he's mumbling.

Food Arts Magazine: May, 1991

When Bad Things Happen

(Quote from an article discussing the unexpected accidents and disasters which must be handled by restaurant managers)

"... Of all the disasters that can befall a restaurateur, <u>death</u> requires the most sensitive treatment. There is nothing so unpleasant as a customer dropping dead in the dining room. It spoils everyone's dinner...."

When shuffling off this mortal coil
Please, have the good grace not to spoil
The dinner of the diners.

And Sir, if you must give up your ghost
Please, do <u>not</u> disturb your harried host
Don't exit with the entrée.

Oh, my—I see your reservation
Was for a <u>birthday</u> celebration
Rest easy—we'll light a candle.

Food and Drink

Places to Eat
(Excerpt from the *Official Guidebook to the City of Hangzhou*)

> ". . . While dog is considered a delicacy, it will not usually be offered to western tourists . . . ."

When walking about in Hangzhou

Please keep old Rover close in tow.

And don't let Spot out for a stroll

He'll end up in some casserole.

In China, Fido's future's dark

There, a bite <u>is</u> worse than a bark!

Norm Levy

Magna Carta Tea Room

(A sign on a quaint restaurant near the monument at Runnymede in Surrey marking the spot where the Magna Carta was signed in 1215 A.D.)

In 1215 in Runnymede

The barons forced King John to cede

A bill of rights for gentlemen

An English milestone back then

At 12:15 today in Surrey

The luncheon crowd will skip and scurry

To sip some tea and lift a spoon

In the Magna Carta Room

King John—you've come a long way baby—

   . . . Maybe!

Food and Drink

The New York Times

Waiter, A Wine Glass List, Please

"Mr. Riedel, the tenth generation proprietor of Riedelglas of Kufstein, Austria, designs and produces different glasses for different varietals. 'If you use the wrong shape, it's like left half the bottle behind,' said Mr. Riedel."

Is this glass too deep or too shallow?

I pondered as I sipped my Gallo!

Norm Levy

Esquire Magazine: 1975

Great Moments in Dubious History

"Albuquerque waiter Shun Hang Fung suffered burns on his arms, shoulders and upper body when a flaming duck he was about to serve exploded in his face."

    Poor Shun Hang Fung had the foulest luck

    He misunderstood when someone yelled

    "Duck!"

Food and Drink

Cincinnati Downtowner: March 30, 1993
Advertisement

I'm sorry I passed up this scene

Missed the booze and nicotine

Missed the chance to puff and feast

With the foremost smoke ring artiste.

Missed the chance to play my small part

In supporting a dying art

AP International: August 25, 2000

Connoisseurs Try 300-Year-Old Wine

Almere, Netherlands—"The connoisseurs held the ruby vintage up to the sunlight, swirled it in their glasses, and put their noses to the rim. 'It smells like cow dung!' one exclaimed. But so strong was the temptation to sample a 300-year-old bottle of wine recovered from a 17th century Dutch warship that none of the experts on the panel was able to resist . . . 'There's a hint of fruit in it, orange peel, marmalade and caramel,' said wine commentator Lucette Farber, swishing the liquid in her mouth as a fetid odor wafted through the tasting room . . ."

I toast this heroic oenophile

Who managed to flash a knowing smile

While tasting with her practiced tongue

Midst fetid odors of bovine dung.

"Vintage rating" for <u>her</u> I'm thinking

For the power of positive drinking.

Travel

"The World is Your Oyster," is a phrase of Shakespearean origin circa 1600. Today, that world and its oysters are ever more available to ever more people if they can fork over the cash, have the time to spare, possess a tolerance for delays and security precautions, can endure squeezing into small spaces, and above all, enjoy a sense of humor. But, it's mostly worth it.

Norm Levy

Travel

The New York Times: August 8, 1995

Boxer Shorts for Travelers

SAN FRANCISCO — "Richard Branson, the Chairman of Virgin Atlantic Airways, and Nicholas Graham, the founder of the company that makes boxer undershorts, both have to fill seats. Customers who buy five pairs of Joe Boxer underwear can get two economy class tickets to London for the price of one fare on Virgin Atlantic."

Two companies have common cause
They both have seats to fill
The genius of the marketplace
Now works its mystic will
Buy underwear and fly half price
Seems foolish at first glance
And yet it gives new meaning to
"Fly by the seat of your pants."

The New York Times, Magazine Section: March 1, 1995

WINE SHRINES
(Travel Ad)

"Northern Spain—Take the medieval pilgrim backroads to Santiago de Compostela."

In Santiago Compostela
I met a most creative fellah.
He had a brilliant inspiration
About a new form of vacation.
Combine the best of "shrines" and "wines"
The kinship goes beyond mere rhymes.
Let spiritual and spirits meld
For traveling joy unparalleled.
Tired of touring monasteries?
Savor several vintage sherries.
Dazzled by altars clad with plate?
Potent port will alter your state.
If martyred saints make eyes misty
Sip some soothing Lacrima Christi.
Shrines and wines produce a blend
That generates this dividend:
When drinking leads to indiscretion
The next day you can make confession.

The Wall Street Journal

Bladders

(From a section entitled: "Valuable Free Resources")

" . . . Arthur Frommer, the travel expert and author, has published an unusual, if not helpful, guide: 'Where to Stop and Where to Go' . . . [It] identifies museums, restaurants, and tourist attractions in four national parks and nineteen cities where travelers can find a restroom . . . . The guide is designed to help people suffering from a condition called overactive bladder, which affects one in six adults age forty and older . . ."

The urgency of nature's call

Is strong, and engages us all.

Travelers, both first class or tourist

The casual sort or purist

Will put aside standards of clean

To seek out the nearest latrine

Or privy or tree trunk or wall

Or hidden recess in a mall.

Mr. Frommer comes to the aid

Of bladders that don't make the grade.

Of his deeds surely this one is chief

The promise of blessed relief.

Herald Sun: December 7, 2004

Americans Weigh Down Cruise Ship

"Dozens of seats on the world's most luxurious cruise ship have collapsed under the weight of obese American passengers. The chairs on the Queen Mary are being replaced or repaired... [there are] ten restaurants on the ship, so if they are big when they get on, they tend to be bigger when they get off."

"Heavy seas"—a different notion

For cruise ships plying the ocean.

Signal every ship that passes

Keep watch for titanic asses.

Brace all chairs—there's no escaping

Or you'll find more bottoms scraping.

Buffet platters full to brimming

Like sails, will require trimming.

Ships may wallow short of sinking

Stimulating heavy thinking.

Speaking firmly—free of rancor—

Watch your weight when weighing anchor.

Afghanistan On-Line

AFGHANISTAN: THE FRIENDLIEST NATION IN THE WORLD— IF NOT THE UNIVERSE

(Web Site Slogan)

As an old, experienced tourist
I've learned not to act like a purist
When reading most travelogue copy
Well known as indecently sloppy.
But, it takes a most positive stand
To describe this most violence-prone land
As the "friendliest" in the extreme.
I'd guess that a poppy field dream
Induced this linguistic mutation
Or mangled and tortured translation.
<u>Most</u> likely, the poor writer instead
Wrote down "friendly" . . . a gun at his head!

Newsweek: August 30, 1993
(Perspective Page)

The Problem is Where to Go . . .

"'and folks do need to go to the toilet on the way up and down . . .'

Quote of Kenneth Stuart, a member of British Mt. Everest Expedition, studying ways to install a public lavatory on the mountain to alleviate the 'unpleasant odor' lingering around base camp."

Mr. Everest—coldly majestic

May be less than antiseptic

Mid icy walls and frozen dells

Lurk unexpected fecal smells

When climbing up or down the peak

There comes a time for all to seek

Surcease of sorely urgent kind

Compelling one to quickly find

Through glaring ice and snowy plume

A clean Mr. Everest-room

Sports

Whether we play or just watch, sports provide a welcome diversion from the "work" of everyday life. That's why the word "playground" has such generally positive associations for most people. And even when "competition" enters the scene to crank up "play" to "combat," it's a kind that is generally non-destructive and mostly exhilarating . . . and sometimes quite amusing to behold.

Norm Levy

Sports

Yahoo News: April 18, 2005

Qatar to Use Robots as Camel Riders

✉ Email 🖨 Print

". . . In Qatar, ruling sheiks have responded to calls for banning the use of boy jockeys by embracing robots as the best solution . . . About 40,000 boy jockeys, some as young as 4, are either bought from their parents or kidnapped . . . and taken to the Gulf to ride. 'Improve the speed, the weight, the aerodynamics, to reach the ultimate goal of completely phasing out children used as jockeys,' Sheik Abdullah said . . . By 2007, rulers of this energy-rich emirate say all camel races will be mechanical."

Let Allah bless each chastened sheik
Reforming for the children's sake.
Some critics might go on to say
Consider going all the way.
Mechanize the humpback racer,
Introduce a robot pacer.
No spit, no dung, no snorts, no bites
No feeding costs or camel fights.
Computer chips, strong elastic,
Nylon tufts, dun-brown enamel,
Might yield a swift robotic camel.

The New York Times

Tales from the Dark Side of Golf

"The [CBS] network has been dubbing recorded bird sounds into the background of television golf tournaments, and some clever bird watchers figured it out . . . A spokeswoman for CBS Sports acknowledged that recorded bird sounds were sometimes used, but that the practice had ended . . ."

CBS Sports had its bird feathers ruffled

Agreeing to keep dubbed chirping sounds muffled.

Golf comments continue—pompous and wordy

While golfers chirp on about their last birdie.

Sports

The New York Times, March 9, 1999

Power Dressing on the Playing Field

"Penn State University tested hundreds of athletes . . . of all ages, abilities and fitness levels and found that wearing form-fitting shorts, also known as compression garments . . . increased athletic performance by an average twelve percent and by as much as thirty percent . . ."

Who'd have guessed it—one can enhance

Performance with your choice of pants.

The mantra now: "high compression"

Soon to be the new obsession.

Greedy hands of time have beckoned—

Pants squeeze out that extra second.

Norm Levy

The Wall Street Journal

The Peek-a-Boo Look Gets Cold Shoulder from Skating Union

" . . . the skating union . . . came up with a stricter code dictating that skating costumes must be 'modest, dignified, and not too theatrical in nature.' Outlawed are too much exposed flesh, 'excessive decoration and unitards.' Unofficially, the code is called 'The Katarina Rule' . . . During a skating show months before the 1988 Olympics, the voluptuous Ms. Witt came out of a vigorous camel spin only to discover that she had also popped out of her plunging neckline."

Be sure to look before you leap
And guard against tight panty creep
Flatten out those pesky bulges
Consider what Spandex divulges
Take care that when you stop your spin
All your body parts stay in
Too much flesh just isn't nice
Watch out—you're skating on thin ice!

Fashion

Nudists take the "organic" approach to fashion—all natural, with no additives. For most people, however, those are limited choices. Part of "who we are" is "what we wear" and the way that we look to ourselves and others.

The fun thing about fashion, of course, is that the choices are limited only by our imagination, our bank accounts, and our narcissism. And, it's a world of delicious inconsistency. Yesterday's "old" might be today's "new." Designers draw inspiration from wildly conflicted and often improbable sources, from Puritans to porn stars, from birds and flowers, from history and the imagined future. Even "drab" can be "fab," if the right celebrity wears it. Fashion—it's a playground for the imagination—and the ironic observation.

Fashion

(A "warning statement" included in the
product instructions of a new electric iron)

In this cruel, litigious world
The "warning flag" is now unfurled.
"Cautions" offered willy-nilly
Of risks quite real—risks quite silly.
I'll add one to the list of woes
Important when you iron clothes.
(For lawyers this may seem astute)
"Do press a shirt—don't press a suit!"

The Wall Street Journal Online: February 25, 2002

> ## Designers Hope to Coax Back Shoppers With Messy Clothes
>
> "... What's new in fashion this spring? Try scruffy. From Lee Jeans to Kenneth Cole, manufacturers and designers are hoping to coax back shoppers with clothes that look plain-old-messy ... Ragged hems ... and ... $550 jeans that have been splattered with paint ... After seeing sales shrink by almost 7% in 2001 analysts worry ..."

The fashion wheel begins it's spin
"Neatness" is out; "Messy" is in.
For the cool, the hip, the smarmy
The "look" is Salvation Army.
Raggedy hems, paint-splattered jeans
So burn your Brooks and L.L. Beans.
Scruffy is the latest wrinkle
Press in every artful crinkle
This "Messy" call is tinged with panic
"Messy" may <u>not</u> prove messianic.

The Island Packet: January 13, 2008

Tupperware is Out.
It's Time for a Taser Party

"Dana Leigh Shafman . . . talks about the new Taser C2 at a Taser Party . . . . Shafman is an independent weapons dealer who sells Tasers the way her mother's generation sold plastic food containers . . .

Shafman says many of her women customers love that the C2 is small enough to fit into their purses and that it comes in a variety of colors. When it comes to choosing weapons a lot of women want them in pink."

    Forget that Tupperware collection.

    Girls, we are talking REAL protection.

    Not stupid lids that seal so tightly

    But "tazed" intruders glowing brightly.

    And after tea and fruitcake slices—

    Improvised explosive devices!

Norm Levy

Wall Street Journal: June 3, 2005

Going Over to the Dark Side

"... *Bottle blondes are losing some of their time-honored cache ... lately, being brunette has gained a new chic ... 'There is a desire among women to look more authentic in their fake hair color,' says the editor in chief of* Allure *(magazine)."*

Blondes are out while brunettes are in
"Authentic" is the latest spin.
Gold stars for those darker tresses
Brown points for all blonde excesses.
"Authentic" linked to tinted locks
Seems something of a paradox.
But fashion voices dare not say
To be "authentic," keep your gray.

Fashion

The New York Times Sunday Supplement:
November 25, 2001

HOORAY FOR GAULTIER

"The genius of Jean Paul Gaultier's fall couture collection was its splendid ordinariness."

Fashion shows its bankrupt state

Its very core upended

With nothing new on fashion's plate

"Ordinary" equals "splendid!"

The New York Times: November 3, 1991

New Wrinkle to Aged Jeans

"'A robot puts artificial wear on a pair of jeans' knees,' the executive director of the men's fashion association in New York said, reverse snobbery has made such finishes popular. Buyers of pre-worn jeans are trying to avoid the appearance that they have arrived fresh from the clothing store. 'Jeans with localized abrasions,' he added, 'makes the wearer look as if they have been there for awhile, rather than looking as if they just got there'. . . ."

Please, be a friend and wear my jeans

Walk a mile in my shoes

Pack *my* troubles in *your* kit bag

While I just sit home and muse

And while you're at it—live my life

And I'll catch up when I can

I'll have my robot think my thoughts—

I'm a New Age gentleman!

Fashion

The New York Times: December 25, 2001

Retailer's Desperation Sales Fail to Lure Holiday Shoppers

"'Merchandise is not like Merlot,' said the chief executive of Bloomingdale's . . . 'it's not going to get better with time.'"

Most merchandise is not Merlot
And wishing will not make it so
Proclaimed a worldly retail sage
Aware that trinkets do not age
With grace and promise of fine wine
Which justifies an "on sale" sign
Intent of which is to cash in
Before the goods go out of fashion!

Norm Levy

The New York Times: March 17, 2002

Less Than Meets the Ear

"With the revival of [hairstyles, such as] newsboy caps and asymmetrical bobs, it was predictable that the one-earring look wouldn't be far behind. The fashion began resurfacing earlier this year, when Chloe designer Phoebe Philo introduced [a] super sized single rhinestone arrow [shaped] earring."

What genius! A single earring
Frees the other ear for hearing
Rings and beeps, web based crashes
Songs and signals, dots and dashes.
No earring means there's greater space
To screw your cell phone into place.

Fashion

The Economist

Indonesian Coverup
July 29, 1995

"Primitive tribesmen wearing penis-gourds do not fit comfortably into modern Indonesia.... Back in the 1970s the army launched 'Operation Penis-Gourd.' Jogging shorts and dresses were airlifted to the Baliem Valley in central Irian Jaya and distributed to the natives. An American missionary present at one distribution recalls that the next day men were wearing the shorts on their heads and women were using the dresses as shoulder bags."

> A penis-gourd! Pants on your head!
> I see little cause for dismay
> It's another culture's version
> Of corporate "casual day."

The New York Times: September 9, 1991

An "Off-the-Boat" Look of Romantic Thrift

"... for men, a peasant look, or in some cases, an 'immigrant' look, has emerged ... Inspiration has been found in the sepia images of steerage ... wearers look as if they are stepping off the pages of old photo albums ... Workman's sweaters ($155) have elbow patches of suede (which come in four colors). To create a slouchy suit, a shadow striped jacket ($345) can be worn with the trousers, preferably mismatched. A jacket with a hood of soft mud-brown leather with horn buttons ($750) is given a hard-times touch with an embossed impression of coarsely woven hemp hopsack...."

> The togs that Grandpa wore in steerage
> Might qualify him now for peerage.
> (At least bolster self-esteem)
>
> From Ellis Isle to Perry Ellis
> The fashion world has much to tell us
> (Things are seldom what they seem)
>
> That tattered coats and faded britches
> Might pave the road from rags to riches
> (It's the American dream)

Fashion

The New York Times: September 12, 1993

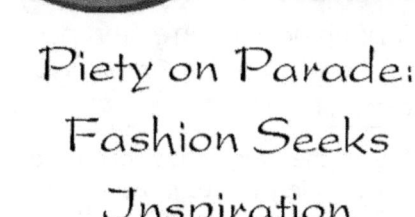

Piety on Parade: Fashion Seeks Inspiration

"The fashionable woman is pictured cloaked in a shroud, shod in high-laced boots worthy of Chaucer's pilgrims and draped in a clutch of crosses . . . Calvin Klein who pares his models down like initiates to a couture convent, and whose Eternity perfume is closed with a cross-shaped stopper, said, 'I look at the robes that are worn by the clergy, the pristine white shirts that choir boys wear, or the way the Amish dress, and it all comes together for me.'"

If you can't live it—then wear it
Take up the cross—you can bear it
Come—play at the fashion charade
Put your piety on parade.
For Calvin it all comes together
Tunics and shrouds for all weather
Who know where devotion may start?
We're all Calvinists—at heart.

The Wall Street Journal: January 5, 2008

> ## Extreme Baggage
> Giant Handbags Are Getting Bigger—And Are a Growing Concern
>
> "One of the biggest fashion trends of 2007 is going to get more extreme in 2008. Some of the largest bags, shown by everyone from Louis Vuitton to Chanel and Prada, now measure up to 2 feet in length . . . the size of a small garbage bag . . . A spokesperson for the American Chiropractic Association estimates that the number of purse-related injuries and sprains she treats has risen 30%. 'When people come into my office complaining of neck pain, shoulder pain and headaches, I go over and pick up their handbag and give it a weigh test . . . it's amazing how heavy they get . . . .'"

Like Marley's ghost hauling its chain

The "Fashionista" suffers great pain—

Backache, neck ache, and even worse

Schlepping her huge, and pricy, purse.

A Zen-like voice booms this rebuff—

"Don't weigh yourself down with your stuff."

Fashion

Label on an expensive tartan design shirt in a Saks Fifth Avenue Men's Shop

Descendants of Vlad the Impaler
Now meekly stick needles in shirts
Both frilly and spartan
But all of them tartan
Plus kilts and wee bonnets and skirts.

Once Wallace and Bruce battled bravely.
There were kings, the clans, the Black Watch.
Now, there's little remorse
When you choose to outsource
(Just avoid the Romanian scotch!)

Norm Levy

Coastal Living, February, 2003
(Excerpt from description of a guestroom)

Termite Tracked Wood Lends Texture to the Guest House . . . A Former Garage

Like mystic alchemists of old
Transmuting baser lead to gold
<u>Designers</u> take discarded trash
Transforming it to ready cash.
The wall is streaked with termite tracks
The ceiling's likely full of cracks
The concrete floor is stained and cold
The air's perfumed with oil and mold.
It's now a place where guests may lodge
Ensconced in some one's rank garage.
It's never old, never tired
When tagged: "Designer Inspired."

Animals

Cute, cuddly, and furry OR ferocious, deadly, and enormous—animals are endlessly fascinating to us humans. Likely we are "wired" to respond to observed aspects of animal behavior that mirror actions and emotions that are clearly familiar to us: anger, sex, fear, affection, parenthood, and the like. The fanciful folks at Disney and Pixar and the Star Wars bunch understand this well. It's always been the stuff of myth and fairytales, ascribing human characteristics to non-human beings. Cultural anthropologists study this, but you knew it the first time your mother read you "The Three Bears" or your Aunt Frances sang "The Eenzy Weensy Spider" as you cooed in your crib.

Norm Levy

Animals

The New York Times: June 6, 1998

Why Are The Lilly Pads Emptying?

"In 1989 in Canterbury, England, the world's leading experts on frogs gathered for their first ever world congress . . . . They realized that they were all seeing the same problem: Their frogs and toads were dying—not just in disturbed habitats, but in the most pristine nature preserves . . . . Today, the case of the dying frogs is well documented . . . but no one knows exactly why they are."

It's a mad apocalyptic
    joke—

Where frogs are just
    the first to croak!

The New York Times: April 24, 2007

Bees Vanish: Scientists Race for Reasons

And now the bees themselves are stung
Hives are empty; the trap is sprung.
With frogs and bees now neatly hexed
Sit back, relax, and guess who's next.

Norm Levy

The New York Times: September 5, 2001

In New Casino Contest Hen House Has the Edge

"Another game is coming to Atlantic City . . . Patrons of the Tropicana Casino and Resort . . . will be able to play one game a day of tic-tac-toe against a chicken. The prize for beating the 15 highly trained leghorn hens will be $10,000 . . ."

It's a very sure sign that gray matter's thinning

When it's man against poultry and chickens are winning.

Suggesting the need for adjusting the border

Twixt fowl and man in the world's pecking order.

Animals

The Cincinnati Enquirer: August 4, 1995

State Fair Cleans Up Its Act
Rules Changed After Livestock Tampering Scandal Officials Say

"Eight of the top animals [at the Ohio State Fair last year] were found to be altered with drugs.... The crackdown began after the grand champion lamb and reserve champion steer were found to contain Clenbuterol, a drug that replaces fat tissues with muscle ..... Procedures to detect tampering have been increased at all fair levels. The champion and grand champion animals in every category must be slaughtered and their tissue tested at a state facility after the competition."

    Society is on the skids

    When pink-cheeked Norman Rockwell kids

    Now sneak into old Bossie's stall

    And dope her with Clenbuterol.

    The Fair's <u>unfairness</u> is complete—

    Now livestock die if they compete.

Norm Levy

Spiegel Online: August 21, 2007

Norway's Moose Population in Trouble for Belching

"Norway is concerned that its national animal, the moose, is harming the climate by emitting an estimated 2100 kilos of carbon dioxide a year . . . equivalent to the CO_2 output from a 13,999 kilometer car journey . . ."

A stand of virgin timber
A sylvan forest glen
A meadow in the moonlight
Far from the sight of men

A rustling in the bushes
A stealthy herd of moose
Swing their mighty antlers
And collectively let loose

A cloud of deadly methane
And ecologic fear
Of CO_2 disaster that
Pollutes the atmosphere

Who sounds the cry of danger
On this distant, Nordic shore
The scientists of Norway
And the Al whose last name's Gore.

Animals

Associated Press Release

Falcons Flocking to the Big Apple—Endangered Bird Thriving in New York

"... A new breed is flocking to town, attracted by New York's highrise residences, and stately churches and bridges, its large number of fat, tasty pigeons.

Experts say that the City's tall structures, many situated near parks or rivers, resemble the falcon's natural cliffside habitat. The bird perches above its prey finally diving down for the kill at up to 200 miles an hour..."

Sharp etched against the city sky

A flock of falcons swoop on by

High above the streets and people

Nesting on a slender steeple

There, they practice bird religion

Based on sacrifice of pigeon

With talons bared, they dive away

Each screeching fiercely: "let us prey!"

The Economist: July 6, 1996

Business This Week

"A chimpanzee in Poland earned a 10% return on investments in the Warsaw Stock Market over three months, beating a good local brokerage. Karoline [the chimp] picked the five winners from 70 tangerines—each inscribed with the name of a firm on the main market."

Some vindictive fiscal jokers

Love making monkeys out of brokers

In Poland, droll investment junkies

Are making brokers out of monkeys.

Animals

The Econonmist (in Brief Section)

Excited bird watchers rushed to Landguard Capitol Point in Suffolk to watch the third sighting this century of Blyth's pipit. Their enjoyment was cut short by a kestrel which chose the pipit for its dinner.

To hell with thee Blyth's Pipit
Damned bird that never wert
I waited near a century
Now you're some hawk's dessert.

Newsweek: May, 1991

Bovine Digestion

"... Each year, Bessie releases 77 pounds of methane into the atmosphere. Cow flatulence makes up more than 2% of worldwide additions to greenhouse gases...."

Now, languid Bessie stands accused

Yet another sordid player

An environmental hazard

Adding to the smoggy layer.

Cows a-mooing in the meadow

Aren't innocent or placid

If we want to cool the planet

Feed our bovines more antacid!

Islandpacket.com

Couple Shuns Scaly Visitor
Published August 10, 2007
Email Article | Print Article

". . . use the peephole. You never know who or what will knock on your front door. For the Lorettas, it was a big 'what' that came knockin' at their Sun City Hilton Head home Friday night. A 6-foot-long alligator pounded on the front door of their Penny Creek Drive home at around 7:45 p.m. . . . 'It looked like he was going to ring the doorbell.'"

Yes, Hilton Head is a charming place

You are greeted here with Southern grace

Neighbors smile—and a little later

"Hi" from your local alligator.

Animals

Education

"Great oaks from little acorns grow" expresses the romantic hope of education to transform and nurture. But too often the realities intrude: access, costs, lost opportunities, bureaucracy, lack of encouragement, and ever new and ingenious diversions. Will we ever learn?

Norm Levy

Education

USA Today: August 17, 2005

College Students Expected to Load Up on Gadgets— Forecast Shows Rising Spending

" . . . Students are expected to head back to campus in the coming weeks with more new laptop computers, iPods, upgraded cell phones, graphing calculators, televisions and more. They—and their parents— . . . plan to spend $8.2 billion on electronics—$700 million more than last year . . ."

We hope that grownup girls and boys

When loading up their adult toys

Remember that the aim of college

Is to load them up with knowledge.

Norm Levy

New York Times
Sunday, December 12, 1995

France Finds a Reading Test Incomprehensible

By MARLISE SIMONS
Published: December 12, 1995

"People of the land of Racine and Moliere, of Hugo and Balzac, of Proust and Sartre, frequently can't grasp what they read, according to a new study that concludes that some literacy skills in France are far worse than those in the United States. . . .

Claude Thélot, a director in the French Education Ministry, rejected the findings . . . He also said that the tests were influenced by what he called the 'Anglo-Saxon culture' meaning that the French were asked 'things the French don't learn' . . .

'For example, one exercise with a recipe asked how many eggs were needed to bake a cake for four people. Then asked how many eggs were needed to back a cake for six. This is not an exercise used in French schools.' Adding a Cartesian twist, he said, 'Anyway, if you make a mistake of one egg, your cake may not be spoiled.'"

    Arcane excuses can't displace

    The egg on Monsieur Thélot's face.

    A Minister of Education

    <u>Must</u> guard the honor of the nation.

    Ring the bell! Sound the klaxon!

    Beware all knowledge Anglo-Saxon.

Education

> *The Economist*
> (Ad in Education section)

Get a College Degree in 27 Days
BS/MS/PHD, etc., including graduation, ring, transcript, diploma. Yes, it's real, legal, guaranteed and accredited.

It's real, it's legal, it's guaranteed
You receive a diploma and a ring
With graduations
Congratulations
It feels like the genuine thing.

It's fake, it's foolish, terribly sad
It's hollow and grim to the core
Just look deep within
Find this singular sin
You're as dumb as you were before.

Norm Levy

Random House Dictionary of the English Language
(The Unabridged Edition, page 771)

"Joukahainen: A Lapp magician who tried to kill Vainamoinen"

I bow my head in heady deference

To this "Joukahainen" reference

The *Unabridged* has every word

To leave one out would be absurd

From Random House, loud cheers and claps

The loudest from literate Lapps!

Everything Else

If you can't find what you're looking for under headings such as Religion, Finance, Politics, Sex, Travel, etc., you just might find it HERE.

Norm Levy

The New York Times: August 15, 1999

Canada Sniffs and Dislikes the Smell

"... *in Halifax, Nova Scotia ... some buildings and businesses have declared themselves fragrance-free zones. The* Halifax Herald *newspaper has a no-scent policy. Employees may not wear perfume, after-shave lotion or scented hairspray at work. School children may be sent to the principal's office if the teacher can smell them....*"

Most folks, if they had their druthers
Would respect the rights of others—
Aim to be satisfactory
In most matters olfactory.
Fragrance is indeed subjective
One can quickly lose perspective.
To guard against undue offence
Apply a dab of common sense!

USA Today: May 19, 2005

Cellphones Top List of What Gets Us Steamed

" . . . In nearly ever gauge of customer satisfaction, the wireless industry scores at or near the bottom. Worse than insurance companies, credit card outlets. Worse than car dealers . . ."

    The infernal ringing

    The burping, the pinging

    The cameras, the buttons, the gear

    All bitching and moaning

    Re cellular phoning

    I say: stick it into your ear!

Everything Else

Plastic or Paper?
(A choice offered to every shopper at the supermarket checkout lane)

Life is full of many choices—

Conflicting pleas, strident voices—

Choose good or evil, ying or yang

Choose peace and light or sturm und drang.

But now there comes a pure delight—

A choice where either choice is right.

Paper? Plastic? Plastic? Paper?

Controversy turns to vapor.

Whichever choice, your goal's attained

To have your groceries contained.

A magic state—no saints, no sinners.

No goats, no losers—only winners!

The New York Times: May 11, 2005

For Train Riders, Middle Seat Isn't the Center of Attention

"... People around New York have a hard time reaching a consensus on many things, but on this—and, really, commuters everywhere, tend to agree: Nobody wants to sit in the center. Transit officials are gradually getting the picture and, whenever practical, are eliminating middle seats . . ."

It's everywhere—a vexing riddle

As people shun the squishy middle.

The "Golden Mean" has gotten meaner

And no one wants an "in-betweener."

The issue swells beyond mere seating

The "center" ranks are fast depleting.

You're right or left or red or bluish.

You're Catholic, Muslim, Buddhist, Jewish.

You poke and prick as best you're able

To have each person show their label.

Yet, on one sure thing we can agree

It's best if you simply think like me.

The New York Times: September 25, 1991

Where Silence Was Golden, Pocket Phones Now Shriek

"... The hushed conversations and simple clicks of cutlery against china at Campton Place, an elegant San Francisco restaurant, were shattered recently by a high pitched squeal that seemed to emanate from one diner. It's happening in theaters, on golf course, at tennis matches, and other bastions of silence, and it's bound to happen more. Last month, the Motorola Company introduced "Microtac Lite," a miniature portable telephone ... that could become ubiquitous as walkmans ...."

Yes, it's true that "silence is golden"

So I'd gladly deliver a fee

To stop the damn phones and the beepers

From polluting the air around me.

I accept the scriptural credo

The one about "my brother's keeper"

But note that the Bible is silent

On my brother's phone and his beeper!

Norm Levy

The New York Times: April 7, 2002
Sunday Style Section

On the Shelf of a Goddess, Gathering Dust

"Fashion glossies, which have shunned unglamorous pursuits like cooking and cleaning, have begun to embrace homemaker chic . . . new coriander dishwasher liquid ($9) and Filigree Fine Fabrics Wash ($19) . . . these . . . are aimed at homemaker voyeurs . . . people who don't want to do their own cleaning. They just want to watch . . . ."

The thought is father to the deed.

Declared an older, stricter creed.

Now, it seems that pressure mounts

To claim it's <u>just</u> the thought that counts.

Do buy the stove, but never cook.

Read the review, but not the book.

Fancy the gloss, cherish the sheen

As long as <u>you</u> don't have to clean.

To <u>do</u> the work might be a botch

It's so much simpler just to watch!

The New York Times: December 21, 2003

The Tyranny of the Standing Ovation

How the Highest Compliment Has Become a Standard Response

" . . .Go to nearly any Broadway house any night, and you can catch a crowd jumping up for the curtain call like politicians at a State of the Union address . . . The phenomenon has become so exaggerated, in fact, that audiences now rise to their feet for even the very least successful shows . . . If almost every performance receives one, then it ceases to be a meaningful compliment . . . "

When "A" is just the common grade,
It signals "excellence" betrayed.
In the halls of education
This is labeled "grade inflation."
When audiences stand and clap
For everyone—it's just claptrap.
In theatre terms, this fake ovation
Should be called "applause inflation."
Perhaps, now is the perfect time
To simply change the paradigm.
Let SILENCE be the indication
Of audience appreciation.
For a performance free of flaw
The audience might stand . . . in awe.

Norm Levy

The New York Times: June 4, 2005

Is Persuasion Dead?

" . . . Is persuasion dead? And if so, does it matter? . . . Is it possible in America today to convince anyone of anything he doesn't already believe? . . . Best-selling books reinforce what folks thought when they bought them. Talk radio and opinion journals preach to the converted . . ."

I see what I see
Don't patronize me
With facts that might alter debate

I hear what I hear
I'll turn a deaf ear
To ideas I don't advocate

I am what I am
I don't give a damn
About thoughts of a different kind

I'll pout and I'll shout
I'll just drown you out
I've told you—I've made up my mind!

Death

Exit laughing? Not usually. But "Death Notices" in major publications are replete with remarkable stories about real people—not fictional creations—the glorious, the notorious, the curious. You can sift through the final telling of obscure facts and events long forgotten, but now recalled as a last exclamation point on a life worth noting.

Norm Levy

Death

> **OBITUARY**
>
> ## MR. WALTER DEWARS, JR.
> ### INVENTOR OF TWINKIES, DIED TODAY AT 82

New York Times, August, 1989

Twinkies—first their proper billing
Golden sponge with creamy filling
Each Twinkies neatly split in twain
All sealed in crinkly cellophane.

I shed a tear, my molars ache
All for Mr. Dewars's sake.
While atoms fuse and nations split
It's he who makes the Times obit
For having whipped up cake and cream
Fulfilling every dentist's dream.

My eyes are lifted to the sky
I ponder Dewars's fate on high
He dwells among those precious few
Who eat their cake and have it, too.

> *The New York Times*
>
> # Hugh Fish, 76, Who Made Thames So Clean the Salmon Came Back
> Published: Wednesday, July 21, 1999
>
> Hugh Fish, a British environmental engineer whose love of pristine rivers helped clean up the Thames—clean enough for salmon to thrive after 150 years—died on May 26 . . . he was 76.
>
> Mr. Fish was knighted in 1989.

> The eponymous Mr. Fish
> Got his cherished life long wish
> And thankful salmon now defer
> And call their benefactor "Sir."
>
> P. S.
> Here is a thought that should remain anonymous—
> At last—a chance to use the word "eponymous"!

Death

The New York Times: March 11, 2002

The Rising Price of the Final Curtain

" . . . Even as the cost of living rises, so does the cost of dying. Funeral costs are climbing according to the National Funeral Directors Association . . . .

Shuffling off this mortal coil

Requires incremental toil

To pay for funeral expenses

Stirring frugal fiscal senses.

With casket prices ever stronger

One might consider living longer.

A "caveat" should now declare

Not "buyer" but "DIER BEWARE!"

Norm Levy

The New York Times

Obituary: W. H. Dalton

"W. H. Dalton, Official Rat and Pigeon Catcher of the City of London, The Ancient Financial District, died today at the age of 79 . . . ."

London's rodents raised their voices
Jeer at men in Rolls and Royces
They gnash their teeth, exclaim "Hooray!"
For W. H. Dalton, official rat and pigeon catcher of
    the City of London, the ancient Financial
    District, passed away.

Pigeons mock from towering heights
And schedule new and deadly flights
For Britain's birdies—joys increased
For W. H. Dalton, official rat and pigeon catcher of
    the City of London, the ancient Financial
    District, is deceased.

<u>ENVOI</u>

Oh, rats and pigeons have your spree
Your bacchanals with fiendish glee
Each shall repent—foul transgressor
For W. H. Dalton, official rat and pigeon catcher of
    the City of London, the ancient Financial
    District, has a successor!

(Previously published in *Varieties*,
New York University humor magazine)

Death

Man Complains Bad Rope Spoiled His Suicide
Fri Feb 28, 2003, 9:21 AM ET

Bucharest (Reuters)   "A Romanian man plans to complain to consumer authorities about the poor quality of a rope which he used in a failed attempt to hang himself. 'You can't even die in this country,' 45-year old Victor Dodol was quoted as saying . . . ."

"Give a man enough rope," one knows,
"He'll hang himself," the saying goes.
This maxim has withstood the test
Except it seems in Bucharest
Where weakened strands of rope denied
A man's attempt at suicide.
"How best to self-inflict my death?"
He muttered when regaining breath.
"To jump, take poison, maybe shoot.
I know—I'll start a legal suit!"

The New York Times: May 5, 1991

G. T. Delacorte, Philanthropist, 97, Dies

"Mr. Delacorte was an avid storyteller in his later years. One day, however, when he was in the middle of an anecdote he lost his train of thought. 'You know,' he said, 'at 92, the memory is the first thing to go.' He paused for a moment and said, 'Well, to tell you the truth, the first thing that goes is sex. Then your memory goes. But the memory of sex never goes' . . . ."

Here's a vaguely bright prospectus
Salient to homo erectus
Grieved about his lost libido
Now comes this simple, hopeful credo
Yes, even when the song is gone
The melody will linger on.

Death

The New York Times: October 11, 1991

Doris Lilly, Author, Dead at 69; Did How to Marry a Millionaire

"... Doris Lilly, the author of How to Marry a Millionaire, and a former newspaper society columnist, died on Wednesday in Manhattan. 'She was never fond of poverty,' wrote Cindy Adams, the New York Post columnist. Ms. Lilly once conceded that her columns were sometimes 'silly' and the people she wrote about were sometimes 'shallow.' 'But,' she said, 'they're pleasant and they smell good and they eat well and drink good wine, and that's all right...'"

Some may dispose of Ms. Lilly

As vacuous, shallow, silly.

And yet, she had lessons to teach

And practiced the lessons she'd preach

"Eat, drink, and be merry..." she taught

Then died—thus completing the thought!

Norm Levy

The New York Times: February 5, 2002

Obituary: Robert Chapman, 81 *Roget's Thesaurus* Editor

"Robert L. Chapman, an editor of Roget's Thesaurus who built a distinguished career on the difference between the right word and the almost right word . . . died in Morristown, New Jersey."

Robert L. Chapman
now is dead.
"Dead" is so harsh—
one could have said
He "bought it" taking
"his last breath,"
Or, "croaked" or "taken
unto death,"
"Cashed in," "checked out,"
"turned up his toes"
At length he found "his
last repose."
One thing is clear:
Bob's truly "gone"
It's nice to know his words
live on.

Death

CNN.com: **March 24, 2002**

Creator of Famed Footwear Dr. Scholl, Dies

"William Scholl, an orthopedic specialist, designed a contoured wooden sandal . . . to exercise the feet and legs, toning the muscles. It was worn for nearly two decades by millions . . . Scholl said it would prevent podiatric ailments."

Clap your hands (and feet) for Dr. Scholl

He toned your muscles, to save your sole.

The New York Times: December 8, 2001

> **Obituary:**
> **George Hansen, 92**
> **Designer of Popular**
> **Swing-Arm Lamp**
>
> " . . . *The Hansen (wall-mounted) lamp, which he introduced in the 1940s, has become known as the classic swing-arm. It is still ubiquitous, illuminating everything from boudoirs to presidential libraries . . .*"

In this puzzling world of quantum effects

It is quaint—but undoubtedly right

To honor a man who swung out an arm,

Turned a switch, and said, "Let there be light!"

Death

The New York Times

Alden Whitman
Obituary Writer in N.Y. Dies

Alden Whitman—Rest in peace

May your soul find sweet surcease.

How rare to see among God's creatures

One who'll practice what he preaches.

OBITUARY

CHARLES DITMAS
CLOCK KEEPER, DIES AT 91

New York Times, January 21, 2002

> "Charles Ditmas, the honorary keeper of clocks at Harvard University . . . believed that each antique clock had a personality as distinct as the one he so assiduously cultivated for himself— with his jet-black dyed hair, Edwardian sartorial style and cherished black bag of ancient tools . . . He was 91, although for years he had claimed to be 110, an odd turn for a man obsessed with the precise measure of time."

A man who loved the clocks of old
Would surely tick a tock if told
The *Times* would print his own obit
In "time" was where his psyche fit.

At ninety one (or one hundred ten)
The heavenly sound of some Big Ben
Tolled the knell and chimed a chime
And Mr. Ditmas knew: "it's time!"

Death

The New York Times

Leo Zippin, 90, Dies Solved Math Puzzle

Published: Saturday, May 20, 1995

"Leo Zippin, a Professor Emeritus of Mathematics at Queen's College, died on May 11 . . . He became known internationally in the 1950s for having helped solve 'the 5th problem of Hilbert.' In a lecture to the International Mathematics Congress in 1900 in Paris, the German mathematician, David Hilbert presented his colleagues with 23 famous puzzlers. They set much of the research agenda for 20th century mathematics."

> *The Times* deserves a bright green Pippin
> For recognizing Leo Zippin.
> While I don't care a fig or filbert
> For problem 5 of old Herr Hilbert.
> So many labored to resolve it
> But—only Dr. Zippin solved it.

Index

A special religious service for broken pins and needles 41
Advertisement for Auto Lease 5
Afghan Quake Victims 87
Agency Will Ask Congress 112
Americans Weigh Down Cruise Ship 152
Amid Revolt, Prices Cut on Bigger Bras 32
Annual Las Vegas Trade Show 26
Astronomy Crisis Deepens 107
Attention People of Afghanistan 54
Bank Branch Bandit Wears Tree Disguise 69
Bank Fires Officer for Gross Misconduct 65
Bees Vanish 179
Bladders 151
Bosnians Divide Over New Talks to Split Country 58
Boxer Shorts for Travelers 149
Brazil nuts 114
Budget Cuts May Foul Sidewalks of Paris 60
Bulgaria Announces Privatization of National Airline 9
Buyer of Aids Patients Insurance Quitting 23
Call the FBI 75
Cellphones Top List of What 198
Charles and Diana Kiss Goodbye 101
China Insists on Naming Living Buddhas 61
Circumcised Foreskin Used in Wounds Test 127
College Students Expected to Load up on Gadgets 191
Confession Makes a Comeback 43
Constitutional Amendment 59
Correction 15
Couple Shuns Scaly Visitor 187
Creator of Famed Footwear Dr. Scholl, Dies 215
Czechs Cut Down on Red Tape by Cutting Watchdogs 50
Designers Hope to Coax Back Shoppers 164
Disney Publishing Unit Settles Suit 19

Don't Forget to Floss 102
Elvis [pictures] on velvet 85
Embarrassed GM to Rename Car With Risqué Overtones.... 6
Excerpt from the book Machiavelli by Ron King 120
Experts Solve Mystery of Unpopped Popcorn...................106
Extreme Baggage 174
Fat Price for Pudgy Gene.. 20
Faxes Sent to God Despite Rabbi's Warning...................... 35
First Gunshot Victim Found in Peru 71
Floss Escapee Sentenced 76
Fly A MiG 29... 25
Fly Has Longest Sperm 116
Get a College Degree in 27 Days.......................................193
Global Conflict 51
Glory of Rome Casino in Indiana to Reopen 10
Great Moments in Dubious History 144
Helms Objects to Funding... 55
How Dentists Sank The Shippers..17
How the Pope Will View Manila... 38
In Afghanistan CIA Gets Creative in Fight for Influence 47
In Kiosks of London 100
In New Casino Contest Hen House Has the Edge 180
In Picking Stocks, Monkey Outshines Big-Name Pros......... 22
India has pioneered a semantic revolution...................... 94
Indonesian Coverup... 171
Is Persuasion Dead?...204
It's Been a Bad Year for Seers 7
Jet Lags..105
Joukahainen 194
Jumbo Paintings Become White Elephants 89
Label on tartan design shirt 175
Last Minor Leaves Montana Ranch 56
Lawyer's In-Court Reading Gets Book Thrown at Him....... 62
Leo Zippin, 90, Dies..219
Lewinsky Visit to Russia Canceled 86
Lonely Hearts of the Cosmos 119
Magna Carta Tea Room...142
Mahanta Votes in Regal Style 57
Make $4000 Per Day Playing Baccarat 11

Man Gets Two Years in Violin Case 70
Markets Have a Funny Way 8
Math Fans To Celebrate Square Root Day........................113
Men Who Use Mobile Phones Face Risk of Infertility 130
Mexican Executive Acquitted of Fraud 16
Middle Seat Isn't the Center of Attention 200
Milestones... 91
Miss America Wants Swimsuits Dropped 81
Miss New Jersey USA Reportedly Resigns.........................92
Moody's Weighs Warning Labels for Its Ratings.................27
More Hotels Try Fewer Sheet Changes................................4
Negative Economic Growth... 21
North Korea Sees Plot After Death of Gift Cows................49
Norway's Moose Population in Trouble for Belching 182
Obsessed in Rio..90
Odd Microbe Survives Vast Dose of Radiation 117
On the Horizon A Way to Write in Thin Air 111
On the Shelf of a Goddess, Gathering Dust......................202
Phones Dirtier Than Toilets.. 129
Piety on Parade 173
Pisa's Leaning Tower Reopens 14
Pizza Hut Billboards 40
Plastic or Paper? 199
Please See That the Perpetual Light is Extinguished 37
Police Find That "Holy Sand" Was Drugs 66
Police Hit with Kangaroo Tails...67
Police Kill Man to Stop His Attempt at Suicide 72
Postal Compost 109
Power Dressing on the Playing Field 159
Pregnant Cheerleaders Bring Turmoil 99
Private Smoking Club at Del Frisco's 145
Prostitution Has Not Suffered Drop-Off 97
Psychic Friends Network Files For Bankruptcy 84
Qatar to Use Robots as Camel Riders............................... 157
Researchers Link Income to Higher Mortality Rates 124
Risk Officers Caught in the Crosshairs................................28
Scandal Shaking Brazilians' Faith in Democracy..................77
Senior Clairvoyants.. 13
Sex Doesn't Sell 93

Six Course Dinner Extravaganza 145
Smokers May Be Ohio's Savior 52
Snap-Happy Crooks Incriminate Themselves 78
Sorry Is the Rarest of Words 30
Spiritualism Embracing Materialism 39
Starbucks Out of China's Forbidden City 29
State Fair Cleans Up Its Act 181
State May Loosen Gambling Rules 53
Steal This Book 68
Study Says Babies Have Math Ability 125
Termite Tracked Wood Lends Texture 176
The Beleaguered Dinosaur Institute Keeps Digging 110
The Hard Task of Reforming Nigeria's Banking System 3
The Most Overrated Books of 2001 88
The Peek-a-Boo Look Gets Cold Shoulder 160
The Problem is Where to Go 154
The Rise and Fall of Civilization 48
The Screech of Tires 134
The Tyranny of the Standing Ovation 203
There and Back Again 98
These Old Stogies Might Be Worth $2,000 Apiece 12
To Punish Thai Police, A Hello Kitty Armband 74
Two British Lordships of the Manor for Sale 24
Uproar Over a Sliced, and Revered, Meteorite 36
Various Headlines 82
Waiter, A Wine Glass List, Please 143
Weapon That Can Obliterate Graffiti 118
When Bad Things Happen 140
When It Takes a Miracle to Sell Your House 31
When Mary Is Sighted 42
Who Would Have Thought Bagels Could Be Dangerous?.123
Why Are The Lilly Pads Emptying? 179
World Bank Beats Breast For Failures in Indonesia 18
Yeast Gene Map Promises Clues to Human Diseases 115

About the Author

Norm Levy's long career with the world's leading advertiser taught him the power of an arresting headline and the value of compressed communication—occasionally leavened by a smidge of humor. He has written riffs on news headlines for decades for publication and for open mike venues. Norm is a published Country Western and Blues songwriter. He has also put his writing and communication skills to work on major Public Service campaigns, and he is a faculty member of the U. S. Marketing Communications College at the U. S. State Department. In an earlier incarnation he served with U. S. Army Counterintelligence. He holds degrees from New York University and Columbia University. He has traveled widely and has worked in thirty-one countries. He now resides with his wife, Joan, on beautiful Hilton Head Island, South Carolina.

www.ingramcontent.com/pod-product-compliance
Lightning Source LLC
LaVergne TN
LVHW051046080426
835508LV00019B/1724